IQBAL

POET AND HIS POLITICS

Riaz Hussain

UPPAL PUBLISHING HOUSE
NEW DELHI

UPPAL PUBLISHING HOUSE
3, Ansari Road, Daryaganj, New Delhi-110002

ISBN 81-85024-23-5

Reprint 1987

PRINTED IN INDIA
Published by B.S. Uppal, Uppal Publishing House
New Delhi-110002.

Printed at Efficient Offset Printers, New Delhi-110028

Contents

Foreword

A biographical book such as this can be written in two ways.

First, formulate hypotheses and select suitable material from the available evidence.

Second, read through the evidence and then arrive at certain conclusions.

I have followed the second course. My conclusions are: Iqbal's socio-economic thought had already been well-formulated as early as 1903, before his first-hand contact with Europe (1905-1908) and much before the Bolshevik Revolution in Russia (1917). In *Ilm-al-Iqtisad* (1903), he had declared himself on the side of peasants, labourers and economically depressed classes and had pioneered the idea of planned parenthood for resolving the problems of poverty and unemployment.

His subsequent passion for economic modernism was, therefore, a systematic outgrowth of his earlier ideas. Nor was his political philosophy unsystematised. He was a patriot as every moral man would be and wanted political freedom and economic prosperity for all the people of India. irrespective of caste or creed. But his first and foremost commitment was to Islam.

Islam by nature cannot be merged with any other creed. It has its distinct social, economic and political structure. As soon as it is amalgamated with any other system, Islam is tarnished out of shape. Iqbal's argument was, therefore, simple—Hinduism and Islam are so distinct that they must have separate homelands in India. There is nothing contradictory in wanting friendship with Hindus, praising their good men, writing patriotic songs, desiring freedom for the whole of India and at the same time demanding self-determination for Muslims. Iqbal, therefore, formulated the doctrine of *Khudi* (militant defence of self-respect) for Muslims which was in direct contrast to Gandhi's *Ahimsa* (maintenance of self-respect by passive means). These two doctrines best symbolise the different outlooks of Muslims and Hindus.

Again there is no conflict in Iqbal's endorsement of socialistic principles and his commitment to Islam. He was a relentless foe of Western Imperialism. Democracy, Fascism and all the political doctrines emanating from Western Europe had one aim : Suck the blood of the poor nations of Asia and Africa. Communism was a reaction against Western Europe's economic exploitation of the depressed people of the world.

The communist ideals—economic justice, social equality and support of freedom movements in Asia and Africa—were nearly akin to the spirit of Islam. The only flaw in Communism was its Atheism.

Thus all the contemporary ideologies were either thoroughly depraved or grossly inadequate. The only choice before the world was Islam which is a just and complete system. In the subcontinent, Iqbal stood in the direct line of such politically clear-headed Muslims as Mujaddid Alf-Thani and Aurangzeb Alamgir. In fact, since Aurangzeb's death (1707), Iqbal was the first Indian Muslim who clearly perceived that Islam could survive in the subcontinent only under an Islamic Government. The ideology of separate Muslim nationality was evolved by him as far back as 1911.

He was among the few Indian leaders, and certainly the only Muslim political leader of his age, who had a truly international outlook, and again the only Muslim leader who thought and wrote extensively about international questions of his contemporary world.

Many of his conclusions on international affairs are valid to this day and the suggestions he proffered are well worth heeding.

To sum up from the evidence I have presented in these pages Iqbal emerges as a staunch Muslim, a consistent political and economic thinker, a warrior for India's freedom and champion of the rights of the poor, an internationalist and a firm believer that only Islam can and will redeem the world from going to pieces.

—Riaz Hussain

Islamia College of Commerce,
Lahore
5 December, 1977

1

Beginnings

Shaikh Muhammad Iqbal was born on 9 November 1873 in Sialkot. His family hailed from Kashmir and like most Kashmiris had joined the ranks of lower middle-class working people in the towns of the Punjab. Iqbal's father Shaikh Noor Muhammad, a tailor by trade, was well-versed in theology and mysticism. Instead of training his sons in his own trade, he sent them to modern schools and arranged the best possible education for them. The elder son, Shaikh Ata Muhammad qualified as Civil Engineer and obtained service in the Public Works Department of the Government of India.

Iqbal studied up to the Intermediate in the Scotch Mission College, Sialkot. He was brilliant in studies and, apart from academic work, was interested in pigeon-flying and wrestling, the two most popular pastimes of the Punjab youth in those days.

In 1895 Iqbal came to Government College, Lahore. Almost instantaneously he became a public figure. Bhati Gate in those days was the hub of intellectual activity in Lahore. Two Muslim dignitaries, Hakim Amin-ud-Din, (a Lawyer) and Mian Shuja-ud-Din, used to hold *Mushairas* (poetical symposiums) in their drawing rooms. Iqbal was attracted to these *Mushairas*, and, encouraged by his admiring classmates he began to recite his poems at these assemblies of the leading literary figures of Lahore. At about this time a social and cultural organisation of Muslim citizens of Kashmiri origin, Anjuman-i-Kashmiri Musalmanan, also functioned in Lahore. Iqbal's friend, Munshi Muhammad Din Fauq, a journalist and ethnographer, was an active member of this Anjuman. Iqbal participated in the Kashmiri Anjuman's activities and at its meetings recited several poems touching upon political and cultural problems of the Kashmiris, including "Falah-i-Qawm" (Welfare of the Nation) emphasising self-help and mutual solidarity.[1] He obtained Master's degree in Philosophy in 1899 and was appointed Mcleod Reader in Arabic at the Oriental College, Lahore.

Between 1901 and 1905, Iqbal rose to all-India fame. During this period he taught intermittently at Islamia College and Government College, Lahore. The social prestige of a college teacher ranked low in the hierarchy of professions (still true today). Positions in the Civil Service and practice of law offered greater economic and social rewards. There was another serious drawback in the profession of teaching which must have seriously inhibited a man of indpendent intellect.

The entire educational system was minutely watched by the British Government. The faculty members were over-ridden by bureaucrats. Freedom of thought

1. See Mehr and Dilawar, *Sarud-i-Raftah*, pp. 80-82.

and expression was limited. This was in direct contrast with the Mughul system which the British system had replaced. In Mughul times schools and academies could obtain generous grants-in-aid without submitting to bureaucratic control.

In order to escape from the close atmosphere of the College staff-room and the repressive arrogance of the educational administrators, Iqbal wanted to obtain a degree in Law. Earlier he had studied law simultaneously with his Master's course in Philosophy. In December 1898, however, he had been declared unsuccessful in the preliminary examination. On appointment as Mcleod Arabic Reader at the Oriental College, Iqbal decided to resume his studies in Law. In 1900 he petitioned the Chief Justice of Lahore High Court to allow him to reappear in the Preliminary examination without attending the prescribed quota of lectures, because he had already done so two years earlier. Justice Chatterji turned down his petition.[2]

In 1901, Iqbal applied to take the Provincial Civil Service examination. The Government Medical Board declared him unfit for service on the grounds of a very minor defect. During this period also he drafted and submitted to the Government of India a memorandum on behalf of the Kashmiri Anjuman detailing their demands and making some queries.

In 1903, Iqbal's elder brother Shaikh Ata Muhammad, then working as Sub-Divisional Officer in the Department of Military Works at Quetta, was dragged into a criminal conspiracy by his jealous rivals

2. Salik, *Dhikr-i-Iqbal*, p. 65.

and colleagues. The charges levied against him were entirely fabricated. Apprehending that Shaikh Ata Muhammad would not get a fair trial, Iqbal addressed a letter to the Viceroy, Lord Curzon, describing in detail the facts of the case. It was an enlightened political instinct which impelled Iqbal to take this step. The Viceroy after due enquiry ordered the Baluchistan Political Agency to put an end to the conspiracy.

Side by side with these public activities Iqbal had for some time been engaged in the study of Economics. In 1903 appeared *Ilm-al-Iqtisad* ("Science of Economics"). Iqbal respectfully dedicated it to W. Bill, Director of Education, Punjab, who had been previously his teacher at the Government College, Lahore. It was the first book on this subject in Urdu and its terminology had been revised by Maulana Shibli Numani. Dr. Anwar Iqbal Qureshi, economist and scholar, has noted. "The freshness of approach and the firm grasp of economic principles exhibited by the young author prompts me to venture the thought that he should have devoted himself permanently to the study of Economics."[3]

In modern times the tradition of economic thought or writing has been almost lacking among the Muslims, save in two instances. Shah Wali Ullah Dihlavi, in surveying the growth and collapse of human cultures and civilisations, had determined the role of economic factors in community life. Later, Sayyid Ahmad Khan, in his Pamphlet *Causes of the Indian Revolt*, had touched upon the economic causes of the

3. Preface to *Al-Iqtisad*, Karachi, Iqbal Academy, p. 3.

conflict.

Iqbal's book was a serious attempt to apply the principles of Economics to conditions in India and offer scientific solutions to economic problems.

It is universally believed that Iqbal formulated his social, economic and political thought only after his first-hand contact with Europe. In certain quarters it is equally forcefully held that Iqbal's social and economic ideas were stimulated only after the Socialist Revolution in Russia in 1917.

Al-Iqtisad, on the other hand, is a living proof that Iqbal's thought of the mature age was an outgrowth and development of the basic concepts adopted by his intellect much earlier.

The first hand observation of European society or the Bolshevik Revolution did not give rise to, nor even stimulate, but confirmed the philosophy of life that he had formulated as far back as 1903.

On landlord-tenant and capitalist-labour polarisation, the following passages from *al-Iqtisad* unequivocally express the ideological standpoint of Iqbal :

"If the wealth of the landlord is not the result of his personal effort, then his prosperity is unjust. In view of this fact some scholars vehemently maintain that this injustice is produced by private ownership of property, which is harmful to the national interest. According to the ideology of these scholars, land is not the property of a particular individual, but should be nationalised. This is a very significant point of discussion, but since this is an elementary book I should avoid taking up this question here."[4]

"The development of culture and civilisation in a country is conditional upon the progressive low rate of profit."[5]

"Some researchers suggest that if the labour is also the

4. Ibid., p. 153. 5. Ibid., p. 166.

owner, there will be no place in Industry for the capitalist and the profit which under present conditions goes into the pocket of the capitalist will accrue to the labour."[6]

After a masterly analysis of the economic process, Iqbal concludes that the entire benefit of increased production should neither go to the landlord, proprietor, industrialist nor banker, but to the worker.

"It is, therefore, proved that increased productivity which is the fruit of worker's labour should entirely benefit the workers. Landowners, bankers and factory-owners *should have no claim on it*."[7]

Iqbal regarded a truly national system of education as the *sine qua non* of economic development. He pioneered the idea of planned parenthood and argued in favour of it on the basis of Islamic theology.

In order to keep the population at a proportionate level, he suggested the following measures :

"Our country is deficient in economic resources. The population, however, is increasing at a rapid rate. Nature, famine and epidemics do play a role in keeping the rising population in check, but we ourselves should also make a conscious effort to control the population level by freeing ourselves from the customs of child-marriage and polygamy. Man's economic well-being demands that he should abstain to the possible extent from the fulfilment of his animal instincts and keep the birth-rate low. This aim can be realised by marrying late (i.e. reducing the rate of procreation), avoiding polygamy and controlling animal instincts."[8]

Iqbal believed that alongwith religion, economic factors play a dominant role in human life :

"There is no doubt that religious principles have played an extremely influential role in the course of human history, but

6. Ibid, p. 178.
7. Ibid., p. 167.
8. Ibid., Preface ; also on pp. 207-208.

it is also clearly established by daily observation and experience that earning a livelihood is the constant concern of man, and it is this concern which quite imperceptibly and unconsciously shapes his external and internal instincts. Reflect how poverty or insufficient provision of necessities of life affect the conduct of man. Often poverty and deprivation so encrust the clean slate of human soul that human morality and culture are completely corroded."[9]

In Iqbal's opinion, "the study of Economics is almost a necessity of life, especially in India where poverty is widespread."[10]

Dr. Anwar Iqbal Qureshi, in his introductory note to the Iqbal Academy edition of *Al-Iqtisad* opines that the study of the book establishes beyond doubt "how sound was the viewpoint of Iqbal on important Economic problems and how, sixty years before, Iqbal had clearly spotlighted those issues which confront the country today. The publication of the book is useful for students of Economics and the general reader as an introductory textbook even in modern times".

By far the most momentous event of these early years was Iqbal's debut in 1900 at the platform of the Anjuman Himayat-i-Islam, Lahore.

It was the formative stage of the ideology of Muslim nationalism in India. The educated classes, both Hindus and Muslims, were increasingly becoming self-conscious in nationalistic terms. This consciousness expressed itself in the struggle for freedom from colonial rule, an urge to march in step with the modern era without letting go of the vital past and the yearning for economic and social reforms based on religion.

9. Ibid., Preface, p. 23. 10. Ibid., Preface, p. 24.

The first nationalist Muslim of the modern era was Sayyid Ahmad Khan. He taught the principle of self-help to Muslims in all fields and launched an educational movement to educate them in modern science and arts alongwith a wholesome training in the principles of Islam. Sayyid Ahmad, however, was not averse to British connexion. In fact, by offering an apologia on behalf of the Muslims of India for their part in the "Revolution" of 1857, Sayyid Ahmad urged that the British should look favourably upon the Muslims and the Muslims should actively cooperate with the British.

Iqbal shared the Sayyid's idea of national self-help for the Muslims, but he did not accept his pro-British stance. Sayyid Ahmad Khan's educational movement inspired many public-spirited Muslims throughout India to form organisations and found schools and colleges in provincial capitals and district towns. One such organisation was the Anjuman Himayat-i-Islam, Lahore. Throughout his life Iqbal whole-heartedly supported and patronised the educational activities of the Anjuman, so much so that he even served for a time as a member of the teaching staff of Islamia College which was being run by the Anjuman. The Anjuman, however, in the early decades of the twentieth century at least was dominated by bourgeoisie, feudal and mercantile classes who were interested in two things :

(*a*) Educating the Muslim youth so as to get them some share in Government jobs and in the professions.

(*b*) To maintain active support to the Government.[11]

From the platforms of the annual sessions of the Anjuman Himayat-i-Islam only pious and well-intentioned speeches used to be delivered.

At the annual session of the Anjuman in 1904 a revolutionary voice rose from the stage. Shaikh Muhammad Iqbal, Assistant Professor, Government College, who had been regularly attending the Anjuman's annual sessions since 1900, recited his poem "Taswir-i-Dard" (the Pain Portrayed). Expressing anguish and burning rage at the sufferings of the enslaved subcontinent of India and lamentation at the absence of peaceful concord between members of various communities, the poem penetrated straight through the hearts of the audience. The metaphorical message contained in the poem "Parinde Ki Faryad" (Plaint of the captive bird), which belongs to this early period, was understood and poignantly felt by the large public, not only in the Punjab, but throughout the length and breadth of India. The period from 1905 to 1909 saw the beginning of bitter Hindu-Muslim clashes in India. The Hindus were deadly against the Partition of Bengal and the provision of law by the British authorities envisaging separate electorates for Muslims. In this era, Iqbal wrote poems like "Sada-i-Dard" (Cry of Pain) and "Naya Shiwala" (New Temple). In these poems he advocated peace, settlement and the forging of united front, not a united nationality (as Western and Hindu writers seem to believe) for freeing the subcontinent from

11. The Anjuman's third objective was to provide, within the framework of the British educational system, some religious instruction in Islam. But this objective was only formally pursued.

the British yoke. In these and other poems such as "Himalaya", the voice of Iqbal was that of a patriot, not a nationalist in the sense in which Congress Muslims were later believed to be nationalists. Patriotism in the eyes of Iqbal was a moral duty. As he said later : "Patriotism is a perfectly natural virtue and has a place in the moral life of man".[12]

That Iqbal was a patriot in the early phase of his life, there is no doubt. That he remained a patriot up to the end is sometimes forgotten. But it must be kept in mind that in the peculiar atmosphere of India patriotism was not necessarily the same thing as Nationalism. The poems in praise of Ram Chandra and Nanak and Ram Tirath are just tributes to religious teachers of other communities, respect for whom is enjoined by the ethics of the Holy Quran.

Iqbal's political verse dating from 1901 to 1905 is characterised by two features : (*a*) his desire to see an independent India with Muslims having adequate safeguards to maintain their national identity and (*b*) his constant endeavour to draw attention to those factors of decadence which caused the decline of the Muslims in India. In his zeal for peaceful atmosphere in India, Iqbal spared neither Mulla nor Brahmin. Addressing the keepers of the Temple and the Mosque, he wrote :

> "Come, let us lift the curtain of apartness once again,
> Tie once more the parted ones,
> Erase the blemish of duality,

12. Iqbal, "Presidential Address delivered at the Annual Session of the All-India Muslim Conference at Lahore on 21 March 1932", reproduced in S. A. Vahid, *Thoughts and Reflections of Iqbal*, p. 197.

A long time hence, the hearts' habitat has
been so desolate,
O, come, a temple new, in this land,
let us raise.[13]

In "Taswir-i-Dard" (The Portrait of Pain) he had said:

"In Love is hidden Liberty, if only you could
see
And bondage is discrimination between you
and me." [14]

To the people of India, Iqbal gave a message of love and peace.

The poem "Shama" (The Candle) depicts the poet as having been lost in the differences of mosque and temple :

"In the Ka'bah and the house of idols,
your glow is the same,
But in differences of mosque and
temple lost I am."[15]

He warned his compatriots :

"People of India, if you do not learn,
you will be no more."[16]

In the early phases of the development of his mental outlook Iqbal was influenced by the thought of the Sufis. He for some time believed in the pantheistic concepts about man's relationship with God.

According to the Pantheistic Sufi doctrine, God permeates everything and all religions lead to God. Islam, therefore, is on par with other religions and can be readily assimilated with them.

13. "Naya Shiwala", *Bang-i-Dara*, pp. 88-89.
14. Bang-i-Dara, p. 71.
15. Ibid., p. 32.
16. Ibid., p. 66.

Almost exactly the same conclusion was drawn by the religio-philosophical conception of Islam created by Western scholars. They asserted that Islam was relevant only to conditions of time and place in which it was born. Consequently, it had ceased to be a living relevant force in modern times. It could, therefore, be readily merged with other communities without harm to itself.

Iqbal became a staunch opponent of this sufistic nationalistic dogma. His contact with sufism was the outcome of his strong desire to interpret anew the religious traditions of Islam and sufism was an important stage in the history of Islamic thought.

A number of poems for children (written prior to 1905) were obviously written with India's political situation in mind.

"Parinde Ki Faryad" (The Bird's Lament), the longing of a caged bird for the freedom of the skies and its nest, bears reference to the greater bondage and deeper yearnings for liberty of a whole continent. His poems instilled feelings of intense patriotism in the hearts of his countrymen. They gave a message of peace, goodwill and hope. The vision of "Hindustani Bachon Ka Qawmi Geet" (National Anthem of Indian Children) is one of universal love and peace. But the "Tarana-i-Hindi" (The Song of India) gained so much popularity that it became the unofficial Anthem of India. Ramsay Macdonald in his book *Awakening India* made special reference to it.

According to an Indian writer the "Tarana-i-Hindi" "remains to this day the best patriotic poem written by any Indian poet in modern times. It comes nearest, in fact, to a truly non-communal national Anthem of India".[17] The message contained in "Tarana-i-Hindi" was not new, only the words were more explicit. India had diversity of religions : each religion was a separate entity ; but diversity did not mean dissension :

> "Religion does not teach us mutual belligerency,
> We are the people of India, and India is our country "[18]

The poem does not preach the myth of the unity of religions, but extolls the value of love and friendship between people of different religions.

Iqbal's early poems contain in embryonic form most of the ideas which later played a prominent part in the system of his thought. For instance, there is the idea that the development of the individual is directly related to his capacity for purposeful action. It is action again which determines the destiny of a nation :

> "'Tis Divinity's decree and creation's mode,
> Who walks along the path of Action is by nature loved." [19]

Iqbal knew the value of action even before the action-oriented West had sharpened his awareness of his own peoples' addiction to lethargy and inaction. He must have learned to believe in action from the Qur'an which "emphasizes 'deed' rather than 'idea'."[20]

17. Iqbal Singh, *The Ardent Pilgrim*, pp. 24-25.
18. *Bang-i-Dara*, p. 18.
19. Ibid., p. 66.
20. Iqbal, *The Reconstruction of Religious Thought in Islam*, Preface, p. v.

It is likely that his own restless spirit played not an inconsiderable part in the evolution of his philosophy of action.

Another significant idea in Iqbal's early verse is that religion does not demand that a man should neglect his material needs. In "Din-o-Dunya" (Religion and the World) the poet says that "religion in fact is the guardian of the material world".

Sayyid Ahmad Khan's message to the poet was :

To teach religion in the world,
if this be your aim,
Do not teach your nation that
the world they should disclaim.[21]

This idea later became the pillar of his polical philosophy—that religion was not a private, individual, exclusively other-worldly affair. There is no bifurcation between individual and collective life, religious and temporal concerns, church and state. The spiritual and material life of man is one organic whole. In the search for one poem which best symbolises the first phase of Iqbal's poetic career, the choice may well fall on the "Temple of Love".

Commenting on this poem the famous English novelist and man of letters E. M. Forester says :

"The glory of the courtyard from Mecca shall inhabit that temple ; the image on its shrine shall be gold, inscribed Hindustan, and it shall wear both the Brahmin thread and the Muslim rosary, and the Muezzin shall call worshippers to prayer upon a horn."[22]

E. M. Forester makes out as if Iqbal was propound-

21. *Bang-i-Dara*, p. 24.

22. E. M. Forester, "the Poetry of Iqbal", *The Atheneum*, 5-10 December, 1920, p. 804.

ing another *Din-i-Elahi*, containing elements of Hinduism and Islam. Such a faith might well have destroyed the distinct identity of either faith, which would have been tolerated neither by Hindus nor Muslims, as Akbar's experiment showed.

Iqbal's temple is in India, but it is not of India. The Temple is raised to love, which transcends the images in which it is expressed. It symbolises the universal Love which is the central purpose of Islam.

In 1905, Iqbal proceeded to Europe for higher studies. He studied in both Britain and Germany. In London, he joined Lincoln's Inn to qualify for the Bar. At Trinity College, Cambridge, he enrolled as an undergraduate student to earn a Bachelor of Arts degree. At Cambridge he came into contact with Drs McTaggart, Nicholson and Browne, the first a philosopher and the latter two eminent Orientalists. The Munich University allowed him to submit his thesis "The Development of Metaphysics in Persia" to Professor F. Hommel in English and exempted him from mandatory stay of two terms at the campus. The dissertation was published in 1908 in London and was dedicated to Porfessor Arnold.

In 1906, the All-India Muslim League had been established in India. Two years later in London (May 1908) the British Committee of the All-India Muslim League was inaugurated under the Presidency of Syed Ameer Ali (Former Judge of the Calcutta High Court and author of scholarly works on Islamic law and history *The Spirit of Islam* and *A Short History of the Saracens*. Iqbal took prominent part in the proceedings of the Committee and was elected member of its Executive Board. He was also nominated to a Sub-Committee to draft the rules and regulations for the All-India Muslim League Committee in Britain. With the exception of a brief interruption Iqbal maintained his relationship with the All-India Muslim League throughout his life.

There is a widespread myth that Iqbal's thinking was basically altered by his contact with the Western civilization. This is not true. Iqbal remained rooted in Islam, though he was moved under Western impact to reconstruct Islamic thought. Europe crystallised his ideas. Coming face to face with a society so different from his own, he had an opportunity to compare the modes of living and the systems of values he saw in the East and the West. Europe sharpened his realisation that life must be spent in purposeful action. His friend and confidant Shaikh Abdul Qadir tells us that during his stay in Europe Iqbal had thought of giving up poetry and turning to more sturdy pursuits. Abdul Qadir and Thomas Arnold, however, pleaded with him not to abandon poetry, for his genius could best serve his nation through the Muse. Iqbal accepted their pleas.[23]

The Western scene impelled Iqbal to develop a rational basis for his beliefs. He reaffirmed the importance of *Ijtihad*. His commitment to Islam as the only means of achieving his ideals deepened. Whatever fascination he had felt in his early youth for sufism now evaporated from his mind. The sufi

23. *Bang-i-Dara*, Preface by Shaikh Abdul Qadir.

doctrine stressed the validity of all religions ; Iqbal now came to believe in the rationality of Islam only.

Kant, Leibniz, Fichte, Bergson, and several other Western philosophers had a serious influence on Iqbal. Hegel's dialectics were an important element in shaping the ideas that became the basis of Iqbal's reconstruction of Islamic thought. Iqbal did not borrow the philosophical systems and definitions of Western philosophers. He used only their method of research and their approach to the various phenomena of Nature and society. An interesting case in point is that of Nietzsche. Like Nietzsche, the man-personality (Ego) is at the centre of Iqbal's philosophy. Again, as with Nietzsche's Superman, the Ego meant striving towards constant action. But Iqbal's evaluation of the relationship of man to God and to society was in direct contrast to Nietzscheism. In fact, Nietzscheism as a whole was anathema to Iqbal. In his quest to reconstruct Islam, Iqbal rejected blind acceptance of the ideas of the West.

"This new wine (Western civilisation) will weaken the mind still further. This new light will only intensify the darkness".[24]

The *bourgeois* culture of the West lacked love, which is the essence of humanity. The heart (repository of love and the seat of true knowledge) had been displaced in the West by the mind (the seat of reason, thought). Iqbal realised that the West primarily fosters materialistic qualities and the East primarily develops spiritualistic qualities. "The conscience of the West is commercial, that of the East monkish," Iqbal wrote in *Armaghan-i-Hijaz*

24. S. M. Ikram, *Modern Muslim India and the Birth of Pakistan*, p. 165.

("The Gift of Hijaz").

Iqbal berated the West for its extremist approach to Matter and Reason, and the East for its exclusive concern with spirit and mysticism. About the Western scientist, Iqbal said :

"All that God has marked him by
Is the Speculative Eye."

Again :

"The scientists embellish the outer form of the dead body,
They possess not the Hand of Moses nor the Breath of Jesus.
My heart sees nothing (of value) in this knowledge,
And it yearns for wisdom of another sort."

While Iqbal chastised the Western scientist for being all reason and no love, he also chastised the sufi for being all love and no reason :

"You are looking up to the world of miracles.
[he says to the sufi]
While I have an eye on (daily) events.
There is nothing strange if your eye may change it.
This world of possibilities is inviting you."

Iqbal saw the ineluctable end of European civilisation on moral grounds :

"The culture of Europe pits heart and intuition against one another,
The soul of such a culture cannot remain virtuous.
What is not clean in spirit cannot achieve,
A clear conscience, lofty thoughts or good taste."[25]

After the decline of European culture Iqbal saw a new world rising from the Soul of Islam :

"In the soul of the Muslim, too, is seen a similar restlessness. . . .
Strangely, divinely ; its meaning cannot be told by the tongue.

25. *Ḍarb-i-Kalim*, p. 69.

Watch ! from this ocean floor——what new portents shall
burst !
Watch ; in this azure vault—what new colours shall
spring" .[26]

Iqbal believed that spirit and intellect, reason and revelation are part of the same plan, though they differ in function and importance. This has given rise to a misconception among Western writers on modern Islam that Iqbal was opposed to intellect and scientific inquiry. W. Cantwell Smith asserts that Iqbal was anti-intellectual : "essentially as a revolt against modern capitalism."[27]

Smith's suggestion is naive, because no connection between intellect as Iqbal conceived it and capitalism can be established. In the view of the Qur'an (in which Iqbal implicitly believed) intellect was a gift of God which gave man the power to form concepts and thus raised him above the angels.[28]

Iqbal's conception of intellect is of prime importance in his philosophic system. The chief influences which moulded it were religious and philosophical not political. The political practice of the West did strengthen Iqbal's belief that intellect alone was not enough, but he did not arrive at that belief because of what he observed.

Iqbal's literary output during his three years' stay (1905-1908) in Europe reveals only a few new strands of his developing thought.

First is his revulsion from the glamorous and

26. "Masjid-i-Qurtaba" : (The Mosque of Cordova), *Bal-i-Jibril* p. 13.

27. W. Cantwell Smith, *Modern Islam in India*, p. 113.

28. Qur'an, II, 28-31 ; Iqbal, *The Reconstruction of Religious Thought in Islam*, p. 13.

materialistic West. The West, in his opinion, intoxicates rather than enlightens :

"The European tavern-keepers' wine brings Jubilee,
It has not Sorrow's ecstasy :
Give home-brewed wine to me."

Iqbal's mind turned to thinking philosophically about the nature of the Islamic community. Political problems in the sub-continent did not loom so large before his eyes. He began to ponder over the more fundamental issues like position of the individual in society :

"The life of the individual is contingent,
The life of the community is real,
Sacrifice yourself for your community,
Burn the magic of the illusory."[29]

Perhaps the most significant theme in the poetry of this period is that Islamic nationality is a "pure idea ; it has no geographical basis." The Prophet of Islam (peace and blessings of Allah be on him), says Iqbal, taught "What determines the bounds of our nation is not territorial unity."[30]

The Islamic concept of nationality is above parochial nationalism. It embraces the whole world. The nation of Islam is composed of individuals who believe in One God and His Prophet Muhammad (peace be on him) and order their lives according to the injunctions of Islam, no matter where they live, whatever their colour or racial and linguistic affiliation.

It was under the impact of this idea of Islamic nationalism that Iqbal considered it impossible to impose any kind of unity on the naturally ill-adjusted

29. *Bang-i-Dara*, p. 138.

30. Ibid., p. 144 also "Islam as a Moral and Political Ideal", in S. A. Vahid, Ed., *Thoughts and Reflections of Iqbal*, pp. 29-55.

nationalities of India. His mind, accordingly, concentrated more and more on the Muslims.

"The creators of sects in India are acting like Azar ;
Protecting yourself from idols,
Become the dust of the way to Hejaz."[31]

Soon after his return to India (1908) Iqbal wrote :

"...Islam is something more than a creed, it is also a community, a nation. The membership of Islam as a community is not determined by birth. The basis of Muslim nationality combines the real and the ideal, the concrete and the abstract."[32]

In 1909, he categorically stated :

"The vision of a common nationhood for India has a poetic appeal, but looking to the present conditions and the unconscious trends of the two communities, appears incapable of fulfilment."[33]

Iqbal now conclusively established the most important idea in his political philosophy—the extra-territorial, supranational character of the Islamic community.

It is generally held by the historians that Iqbal propounded the concept of a Separate Islamic State in the Indian subcontinent for the first time in his Presidential Address delivered at the Annual Session of the All-India Muslim League at Allahabad on 29 December 1930.

But while looking through the Report on the Census of India 1911, XIV, 162-64, I have come across some extracts from a lecture by Iqbal entitled, "The Muslim Community". I have not been able to trace the full text of the lecture in any of the Antholo-

31. *Bang-i-Dara*, p. 138.
32. Vahid., Ed., op. cit, pp. 50-51.
33. Javid Iqbal, Ed., [Iqbal] *Stray Reflections*, p. 21.

gies of Iqbal's writings published so far. The compilers of the Census Report also fail to mention where the lecture was delivered or from which published source they had gleaned the extractions. This fragmentary piece of Iqbal's writing is of great significance as it clearly shows that Iqbal had urged the formation of a separate Muslim homeland in India as the only guarantee for the preservation of Muslim religion and civilisation in the subcontinent as early as 1911.

Iqbal's main theme in this lecture is that after Alamgir's death (1707) the parting of ways between the Hindus and the Muslims has become imperative and in the face of Hindu forwardness Muslims can only preserve their national life and culture by modelling their individual characters on the personality of Alamgir and adopting his political and religious programme.

The British Census Commissioners in 1911 evidently did not fully realise the import of Iqbal's remarks and merely looked upon his thesis as of no more than philosophical and academic interest. In an introductory note to these quotations from Iqbal, the Commissioners wrote:

"The basic principles of Islam are contained in the aphorism [Kalima] La Ilaha-il-Allah-o-Mohammad-ur-Rasul Allah (There is none but God and Mohammad is His Prophet). The remarks on this great religion contained in Paragraphs 651 and 654 to 686 of the Census of India Report of 1901, leave little to be added, but a few quotations from the writings of a philosophically inclined Indian Mohammadan gentleman will throw some light on the present state of Islam as viewed by cultured minds of the East".

From the fragmentary report of the Allama's lecture on "Muslim Community" given in the Census the following summary of the author's main ideas may be made.

Iqbal deals with the definition of 'Muslim Community' under three heads:

(1) The general structure of the Muslim community.
(2) The uniformity of the Muslim culture.
(3) The type of character essential to a continuous life of the Muslim community.

Basic Principle

Under the first heading the Allama remarks:

"It is not the unity of language or country or the identity of economic interest that constitutes the basic principle of one nationality: It is because we all believe in a certain view of the universe, and participate in the same historical tradition that we are members of the Society founded by the Prophet of Islam."

In elaboration of the concept of the Muslim society, the Allama proceeds to say.

The point which I wish to stress is that Islam has a far deeper significance for us than merely religion; it has a peculiar national meaning so that our communal life is unthinkable without a firm grasp of the Islamic principle. *The idea of Islam is, so to speak our eternal home or country in which we live, move and have our being. To us it is above everything else as England is above all to the Englishman and 'Deutschland Uber. Alles' to the German.*

The implication of the sentences in italics in the perspective of later history, is clear beyond doubt.

Coming to the second point, the uniformity of Muslim Culture, Iqbal observes:

"In order to become a living member of the Muslim Community, the individual, besides an un-conditional belief in the religious principle must thoroughly assimilate the Culture of

Islam. The object of assimilation is to create a uniform mental outlook, a peculiar way of looking at the world, a certain definite stand-point from where to judge the value of things which sharply defines our community and transforms it into a corporate individual giving it a definite purpose and ideal of its own."

Having defined the uniform character and separate entity of the Muslim Nation, the Allama proceeds to identify the future aspirations of the Muslim Community and the only political solution which can guarantee its continued existence on the sub-continent of India.

The passage relating to the third heading "The type of character essential to a continuous national life of the Muslim Community" bears full quotation:

The modern sociology teaches us that the moral experience of nations obeys certain definite law. In primitive Society where the struggle of existence is extremely keen and draws more upon man's physical rather than intellectual qualities, it is the valiant man who becomes an object of universal admiration and imitation, when, however, the struggle relaxes and the peril is over, the valorous type is displaced, though not altogether, by the convivial type, which takes a due share in all the pleasures of life and combines in itself the virtues of liberality, generosity and good fellowship. But, then, these two types of character have a tendency to become reckless, and by way of reaction against them appears the third great type which holds up the ideal of self-control, and is dominated by a more serious view of life.

'In so far as the evolution of the Muslim Society in India is concerned, Timur represented the first type. Babar combined the first and the second, Jahangir embodied pre-eminently the second, while the third preshadowed in Alamgir, whose life and activity forms, in my opinion, the starting point in the growth of Muslim nationality in India. If it is our aim to secure a continuous life of the community in India we must produce a type of character identical to that of Alamgir, which at all costs holds fast to its own ; and while it readily assimilates all that is good in other types, it carefully excludes from its life all that is hostile to its cherished traditions and institutions. A careful observation of the Muslim Community in India today reveals the point on which the various lines of the moral experience of the community are now tending to converge."

And what was this point on which the various lines of the moral experience of the Indian Muslims were tending to converge? Every word of the Allama's lecture read in cold print, even without the hindsight provided by subsequent history, unmistakably reveals the fact that he had presented the idea of a separate Muslim homeland in India almost twenty years prior (1911) to the date (1930) when he is commonly credited by the historians to have enunciated it.

Iqbal was not merely demanding a territorial state, but the establishment of an ideal.

Apart from being alien to the spirit of Islam, territorial nationalism was open to gross misuse. It was, for instance, a weapon of European Imperialism which destroyed the unity of the Muslim world :

"I have been repudiating the concept of nationalism since the time when it was well known in India and the Muslim world. At the very start it had become clear to me from the writings of European authors that the Imperialistic designs of Europe were in great need of this effective weapon—the propagation of the European conception of nationalism in Muslim countries—to shatter the unity of Islam in pieces."[34]

Another drawback of Nationalism was that it promoted deadly wars :

"Look at the history of mankind ; it is an unending

34. "Shamloo," *Ed., Speeches and Statements of Iqbal*, p. 224.

succession of deadly combats, blood feuds, and internecine wars. Now the question arises as to whether in these circumstances it is possible to bring forth a community the basis of whose collective life will be peace and goodwill."[35]

Iqbal believed that only the Islamic *Millat* was such a nation and that "the ideal territory for this nation would be the whole Earth".

Such an idea was found most distasteful by European critics. For instance, Dickinson, in reviewing Iqbal's *Asrar-i-Khudi* (*The Secrets of the Self*) said :

"Thus, while Mr. Iqbal's philosophy is universal, his application of it is particular and exclusive. Only Muslims are worthy of the Kingdom. The rest of the world is either to be absorbed or excluded."[36]

Iqbal's answer to this criticism was as follows :

"Nor is the spirit of Islam so exclusive, as Mr. Dickinson thinks. . . . In the interests of a universal unification of mankind the Quran ignores their minor differences and says, Come let us unite on what is common to us all !' . . .

"All men and not Muslims alone are meant for the Kingdom of God on earth, provided they say good-bye to their idols of race and nationality, and treat one another as personalities."[37]

Finally, we must consider the question : How is it possible to reconcile Iqbal's condemnation of Nationalism to his personal commitment to Muslim nation's struggle for freedom in India ? The question is not as complicated as it seems. In the first place, Iqbal recognised that "the idea of nationality is certainly a healthy factor in the growth of commu-

35. Iqbal. *Rumuz-t-Bekhudi*, Preface, quoted in S. A. Vahid, *Iqbal : His Art and Thought* (1959), p. 237.

36. Dickinson, "Review of the Secrets of Self by Muhammad Iqbal," *The Nation* (London) 24 December 1920, p. 458.

37. Reproduced in S. A. Vahid, *Thoughts and Reflections of Iqbal*, p. 99.

nities."[38]

Secondly, Iqbal believed that it was not always necessary to refute nationalism, because it was not inconsistent or incompatible with Islam.

". . . Nationalism in the sense of love of one's country and even readiness to die for its honour is a part of the Muslim's faith ; it comes into conflict with Islam only when it begins to play the role of a political concept and claims to be a principle of human solidarity demanding that Islam should recede to the background of a mere private opinion and cease to be a living factor in the national life. In Turkey, Iran, Egypt and other Muslim countries it will never become a problem. In these countries Muslims constitute an overwhelming majority and their minorities, i.e., Jews, Christians and Zoroastrians, according to the law of Islam, are either 'People of the Book' *or 'like the People of the Book' with whom the law of Islam allows free social relations including matrimonial alliances.* It becomes a problem for Muslims only in countries where they happen to be in a minority and nationalism demands their complete self-effacement. In majority countries Islam accommodates nationalism ; for there Islam and nationalism are *practically identical ;* in minority countries it is justified in seeking self-determination as a cultural unit. In either case, it is thoroughly consistent with itself."[39]

Iqbal demanded self-determination for the Muslims, and political and territorial independence is always explicit in the concept of self-determination. Political power for Iqbal was a means to an end and the end was the preservation of Muslim identity in India. In 1930, he suggested the scheme of a Muslim State in India. All his life the territorial and administrative unity of India appeared to him detrimental to the cultural identity of the Muslims. There

38. J. Iqbal, Ed., op. cit., p. 95.
39. Vahid, *Ed., Thoughts and Reflections Iqbal*, pp. 287-88.

is no doubt that if Iqbal had been spared to live ten years longer he would have approved of the Partition idea.

In 1911, Sir Sultan Muhammad Khan Agha Khan III toured the sub-continent of India to collect funds for raising the College at Aligarh to the level of a University. Iqbal wholeheartedly supported the idea of a separate Muslim University in India. By speech and action he exhorted the Muslims of the Punjab to make large donations to the project.

In the early part of this century the centre of intellectual activity in Lahore was Bazm-i-Urdu, which used to hold its weekly meetings alternately in Barkat Ali Muhammadan Hall, outside Mochi Gate and Habibia Hall, Islamia College, Railway Road, Lahore.

Its patrons were Nawab Haji Fateh Ali Khan Qizilbash, Munshi Mahboob Alam Editor, *Paisa Akhbar*, Munshi Shafi-Ullah, Editor *Millat*, Maulvi Muhammad Abdullah, Second Master Central Model School, Haji Mir Shams-ud-Din, Munshi Muhammad Din Fauq, Justice Shah Din Hamayun, Nawab Zulfikar Ali Khan, Khwajah Kamal-ud-Din, B.A., Pleader, and Iqbal himself. Throughout 1911 the call of raising Aligarh College to the status of a university was vibrating through Muslim India. It was intended to collect a fund of Rupees Twenty Lakh for this purpose and to request King George V on the eve of the ensuing Delhi Durbar to grant charter for establishing Aligarh Muslim University. A fund-raising deputation under the leadership of His Highness Sir Sultan Muhammad Khan Agha Khan III was due to arrive in Lahore shortly. To mobilise public support for this cause, the Bazm-i-Urdu held a public meeting on the evening of 19 February 1911 at Habibia Hall, Islamia College, Railway Road.

Iqbal was one of the principal speakers. A minute report of his speech was sent to Muslim newspapers by the Bazm's Secretary, Ghulam Muhammad Amritsari, and was published in the *Paisa Akhbar*, Lahore, 28 March 1911. In this speech, to begin with, Iqbal gave a lucid and impressive definition of Muslim nationhood, which is exactly the same as is recorded in his article quoted in the Census of India Report 1911. The implied argument is simple and clear. Muslims are a nation. Nations, big or small, are equal. Muslims, therefore, must preserve their separate religious, cultural, and political identity. He then proceeds to touch on a point which few Muslim scholars since then have bothered to study or investigate further. Many have asked the agonising question : what it was that led the Muslims to surrender to the West their intellectual initiative in arts and sciences ? But few have studied enough to frame an answer. There is evidence in this speech that Iqbal was the earliest intellectual of the Muslim East who investigated the subject and found an answer. It must be noted that the text of the speech or any reference to it is not to be found in extant sources, save one. Following is the verbatim translation of the report of Iqbal's Urdu speech as published in the *Paisa Akhbar*, Lahore:

"At the grand public meeting of Bazm-i-Urdu held on tne evening of 19 February, Dr Shaikh Muhammad Iqbal, M.A.,

Ph.D., Barrister-at-Law, made a speech on 'Muhammadan University' which was scholarly and solid. The chief merit of this speech was that to the young people who are enamoured of modern civilisation it proved in an eminently rational and philosophical manner the superiority of the principles of Islam and each word of it evinced true zeal of the speaker for the glorious progress of Islam in the world.

"First of all, Shaikh Sahib stated that every nation has a standard of nationality, and it varies from nation to nation. For instance, one nation makes her country the standard of her nationality another nation regards the language and yet another common ancestry as the standard of nationality. He said that, for example, their country is the standard of nationality for the Englishmen. Each time you ask an Englishman, "Why are you called English ?" he will reply, "I am English because I am a resident of England." But ask a Muslim, "Why are you a Muslim?" and he cannot cite the name of a particular country, for neither Arabia, nor Tartar, nor China, nor India is his special country. Similarly, a Muslim is not a Muslim because he speaks a particular tongue, nor are Muslim descended from a common ancestry.

"Upon consideration the only right answer one could arrive at is that there is one common qaulity among Muslims which is the basis of their identity as a Muslim nation and that is their belief in the unity of God.

"The 'Iman-fi-Tauhid' (Faith in one God) is the only common denominator among the Muslim people.

"Faith is related to the soul or heart, said the speaker; in other words belief in one God is a state of the heart, which is an invisible and immaterial phenomenon in contrast to the standards of nationality adopted by other people, which are all material and physical. From this the speaker derived the point that the standard of nationality subsisting among other people such as country, etc., is external to the body. For instance, when an Englishman lands in India his nationality is left seven thousand miles behind. But the Muslims' standard of nationality exists in his own body. Wherever a Muslim goes, his nationality travels with him. As a rule, the speaker said, a man seldom forgets a thing which can be seen or touched; but he has a tendency to forget soon an invisible and spiritual phenomenon.

"The nationality of Muslims, therefore, stood in great danger of extinction since it was ultra-sensory. Hence it was that the teacher of Islam (peace and blessings of Allah be on him) enjoined the duty of commemorating the Unity of God upon every Muslim at the time of waking up at dawn, during the day's business, on arrival at home in the evening and before going to bed at night. In addition, he (peace and blessings of Allah be on him) prescribed a prayer for each movement that a man is obliged to make : arising, walking, sitting down, commencing a meal, etc., so that the Muslims may never forget the standard [of their nationality].

"The existence of each nation depends on its standard of nationality and the need to protect it was imperative, for which reason the Holy Prophet (peace and blessings of Allah be on him) took adequate measures in the above manner.

"Muslim faith, said the speaker, has two clauses : belief in one God and Prophethood and secondly, knowledge of one's own society, culture and polity. A Muslim becomes a Muslim when he adheres to both these clauses. Although the first of these clauses is the basic tenet of Islam, yet even if we do not regard the denial or absence of the second clause as a defect in faith we shall certainly agree that without it no one can claim to be a perfect Muslim.

"Proceeding, the speaker gave religious arguments to establish the importance of knowledge. The first proof of the importance and eternal value of knowledge that the teacher of Islam (peace and blessings of Allah be on him) gave was that he (peace be on him) ordered the release of the literate heathens taken prisoner in the Battle of Badr on one condition : that they should teach reading and writing to the illiterate among the Muslims.

"The speaker went on to state that first of all Ibn Abbas (God be pleased with him) in the reign of Ali Murtaza (Allah be pleased with him) opened a school in Mecca in which lessons were given on Qur'an and *Hadith*. Later,

Hadrat Umar-bin-Abdul Aziz (Allah be pleased with him) founded the Nizamiyah College. This college produced philosophers of the calibre of Sheikh Sa'di. Illustrating his point, the speaker recited a verse of Sa'di.

Subsequently Mustansariya College was established. But both these colleges were not universities in the modern sense. At last the Muslims set up a large university, the university of Cordova, in Spain.

The Christians flocked to this university from all corners of Europe and benefited from it.

"On the model of Cordova University, the Christians at last established a university in Paris, which is still functioning.

"By this example the speaker pointed out that the idea of a university was first conceived by Muslims and Christians borrowed it from them. The speaker said that the most conspicuous feature of the Paris University was that Arabic was a compulsory subject in its curriculum. Why was it so? Because at that time Arabic was the treasury of all arts and sciences.

"Turning again to the real theme of his talk, the speaker observed that the second clause of Islam, namely, the knowledge of Islamic literature, civilisation, culture, polity is preserved in the Arabic language. But since sovereignty slipped out of their hands and they became slaves of foreigners, Muslims had to learn the foreign tongues. In consequence they forgot their own symbols, the Arabic language and their culture, and the second clause of Islam completely faded out of Muslim society. In other words, that which could make them perfect Muslims became defunct. Indifferent to their own culture, they passed under the influence of the cultures of the aliens and their faith weakened.

"Hence it was, stated the speaker, that modern English-educated youth among whom he included himself became denuded of this second quality of faith. This first of all gave birth to heretical tendencies among them and then gradually turned them into agnostics. The most eminent and wise leaders of the Muslims sensed this danger and came to the conclusion that unless the second clause of faith were adequately protected and nurtured, faith would rapidly deteriorate. The best plan of defence, therefore, was to include in a system of education meant for Muslim subjects such as the Islamic social order, Islamic culture and Islamic polity, and this purpose cannot be achieved without establishing a Mohammadan university. If we have an Islamic university, we can have an Islamic curriculum of education. The faith of the young students learning English and Islam itself can only be preserved in this way."

About this time Iqbal was also moved by the Pan-Islamic ideal. Ideas of existence in India of two nations became widespread among the Indian intelligentsia after the World War I. Iqbal began to be influenced by the teachings of Jamal-ud-Din Afghani. Afghani endeavoured to find in Islam a means of unity for resisting the domination of the West. He also showed that Islam favoured the social progress of the people and that independent development of the Eastern nations was a necessity of the times.

Iqbal affirmed the existence of a separate nation of Muslims of India. At the same time he did not lose his Pan-Islamic sympathies.

Muslim nationalism everywhere has desired a close bond among Muslim nations and the establishment of definite supranational pan-Islamic forms of unity. On the eve of and during the World War I, Iqbal directly tied his hopes for liberation from colonial dependency to Pan-Islamic solidarity and the caliphate forms of the liberation movement. This was reflected in particular in his poem "Shama Aur Shair" (Candle and the Poet) written in 1912.

However, it should be remembered that Iqbal never regarded the Muslim community as a religious community only. According to his interpretation, Islam was a philosophy of life, the embodiment of a definite cultural and historical traditions, social and legal institutions, and way of living. He never equated Muslim nationalism with religious intolerance on the one hand, and narrow communal outlook on the other. While upholding Muslim nationalism, he remained an ardent preacher of patriotic unity in the struggle against foreign domination.

In no period of his activity did he deem it possible to set an alliance of Muslims with British colonialists against the Hindus, although Hindus had often collaborated with the British against the Muslims.

On the eve of the World War I, Iqbal co-operated closely with Abul Kalam Azad, Maulana Muhammad Ali and other Muslim nationalists who at that time were simultaneously the members of the National Congress and the Muslim League and their left wings. His activity was aimed, in his own words, at prompting Muslims to get involved in political struggle.

During this period he gave up the teaching profession. He resigned his post at Government College, Lahore, and engaged himself in law practice. In verse as well as in prose he exhorted the people to free themselves from political apathy and participate vigorously in the all India liberation movement. The ideas of this message found reflection particularly in his poem "Tulaba-i-Aligarh College Ke Nam" (To the Students of Aligarh College).

Despite its pro-British orientation Aligarh College had fostered political awakening among Muslims.

The authorities of the College were at this time trying to prevent students from catching revolutionary ideas. They did not want their students to acquire anti-British sentiments. Administrators and professors of this College issued appeals for prudence and support of the British. Iqbal's message was sharply different from these appeals :

> "People are delivering various messages ;
> Mine is different from them all.
> The style of the heart smitten with love is always different;
> Up to now you heard the impotent murmur of fluttering birds in snares,
> "Listen now to a bird who is free—his is a different wail.
> For the moment let the brick of tradition lie in the neck of the pitcher."
> "Out of the fermentation of wine, A new consciousness will arise !"

The poet exhorted the young students to disregard the "impotent murmurs of fluttering birds in snares". He roused them to wage a relentless war against slavery. Nevertheless Iqbal was painfully aware that the poeple of the subcontinent were not prepared to "cast down the brick of tradition" or to adopt the revolutionary methods of struggle. This theme he repeated in many other poetic, philosophical and didactic works. He continued to emphasise the need for an active struggle for freedom and always believed that a new consciousness will inevitably arise.

In politics as well as in philosophy he turned to the reforming role of Islam. In *Asrar-i-Khudi* (*Secrets of the Self*) (1915) and *Rumuz-i-Bekhudi* (*The Mysteries of Selflessness*) (1918) he presented, for the first time substantiation of the necessity of combining the traditions of Islam and their reformation in the spirit of the times with an expostulation of the moral and ethical conceptions of Muslim nationalism and his philosophy of the man-activist. These philosophical poems enjoyed tremendous popularity among the Muslims of India during and after the World War I. They were written, not in Urdu, but in Persian, because Iqbal was appealing not only to Indian Muslims but also to the Muslims of all the oppressed countries. The poems were brought to Maulana Mohammad Ali in jail and, after reading them, he commented : "We soon realised that this was even greater and more enduring than what Iqbal had so far written."

Describing the historical role of Iqbal in the Muslim struggle for freedom, Mohammad Ali wrote :

> "He was the poet of Islam's reawakening in India in the twentieth century, and to no man does Muslim India owe a greater debt than to this modest and retiring barrister of the Punjab."[40]

All the contemporary evidence suggests that Iqbal had become the ruler of the minds of Muslim intelligentsia in India.

The October Socialist Revolution in Russia (1917) exercised a great influence on the national liberation movement of the peoples of the Indo-Pak subcontinent and on the socio-political views of a large section of the educated class. Political leaders in India became suddenly conscious of the role that the working masses could play in the liberation movement. Anti-capitalist tendencies appeared in the writings of many journalists and writers. At the same

40. Mohammad Ali, *My Life : A Fragment*, Ed. Afzal Iqbal, pp. 166-67.

time they believed in the possibility of the development of the peoples of the East in their own original way, according to their own religious and philosophical traditions. Iqbal became the foremost spokesman of all of these strains of intellectual thought in India. In his view the revolution in Russia had inaugurated a new era, "the era of the Workers".

The voice of the worker called out in "Nawai Mazdur" :

> "Let us unite and overthrow the old system."
> [Let us give new regulations to the magicians and their temple.
> Let us overturn the foundation stones of old taverns.][41]

The Bolshevik Revolution in Russia presaged the inevitable doom of the old order. The hearts are surging with revolutionary fervour. The end of the old time has perhaps come !

Under the impact of this revolutionary fervour Iqbal created poetic images of the "Crown" being forcibly wrested away and the Kohkun (the stone mason) demanding the "Estate of Pervaiz" (that is, the ruler).

Iqbal was convinced that after the great changes occurring in Russia, the world would no longer remain the same. The people of the East especially could no longer live under the old system. *Payam-i-Mashriq* (Message of the East) is the representative poem on this subject :

> Now is a time for establishing new systems,
> Let us clean the hearts' state and make a fresh state.
> The Imperial Crown is tarnished, it has been cast away.
> Kohkun (stone mason) came with a chipping hammer in his hands and demanded

41. *Payam-i-Mashriq*, p. 258.

For himself the estate of Pervaiz. Gone is the time of
luxury for masters; of service by the lowly. . . .
If thine eyes know how to see, open them ;
Life is marching to the creation of another world."[42]

The Bolshevik Revolution in Russia was an epoch-making event and it made an intense impression on Iqbal. However, he remained first of all a Muslim ideologist and wanted to realise the goals of socialism through the enforcement of the tenets of Islam.

Payam-i-Mashriq came out in 1923. It contained poems written before and during the World War I. Through *Payam-i-Mashriq*, Iqbal made it absolutely clear that profound socio-economic changes were necessary for the establishment of social justice. But social justice depends on the moral perfection of man. Islam, Iqbal believed, is the only religion which did and will yet reform the moral nature of man. But before Islam could accomplish this task in the modern world, the religious thought in Islam itself needed to be reconstructed. In December 1928, Iqbal went to Madras to deliver six lectures compositely titled, "The Reconstruction of Religious Thought in Islam" at the invitation of the Muslim Association of Madras. These addresses were an attempt "to reconstruct Muslim religious philosophy with due regard to the philosophical traditions of Islam and the more recent developments in the domains of human knowledge."[43]

The Lectures embodied Iqbal's mature formulation of moral, social and political philosophy.

42. Ibid., pp. 230-31.

43. Iqbal, *The Reconstruction of Religious Thought in Islam* (1958) pp. v-vi.

Iqbal believed that to achieve the social and political goal of Muslims in the modern era a reconstruction of Islamic thought was an imperative necessity. Just as Protestantism had reconstructed religious thought of Europe at one time, so must a reformation of Islam be brought about in modern times.

"Today the leaders of the world of Islam were duty-bound," said Iqbal, "to understand the real meaning of what has happened in Europe and then to move forward with self-control and a clear insight into the ultimate aims of Islam as a social policy."[44]

Iqbal emphasised, however, that religion and religious forms of worldview must be preserved to impart true meaning to the existence of human personality and the ideal social system as well as for the exposition of those objective truths which cannot be explained by scientific analysis.

Iqbal set up a distinction between religion and philosophy but regarded religion as superior to philosophy. "Religion is not a departmental affair; it is neither mere thought, nor mere feeling, nor mere action; it is an expression of the whole man."[45]

Philosophy, no doubt, has jurisdiction to judge religion, but religion will not submit to the jurisdiction of philosophy except on its own terms.

Philosophy is bound to admit that religion holds the focal position in the process of reflective synthesis. Iqbal's religio-political doctrine was based on the antithesis between the concept of "God as a

44. See Lecture on "The Principles of Movement in the Structure of Islam" (*Reconstruction of Religious Thought in Islam*, pp. 146-179).
45. *Reconstruction*, p. 2.

personality—a higher 'I' " and the classical Greek doctrine of "God as a Substance".[46]

God is eternally living and eternally creating. Nature and society are undergoing a dialectic process of development. God did not create things as they appear to us. He created only the atoms of which they consist.[47]

The creative process initiated by God does not cease. Fresh atoms come into being every moment. Thus the universe is constantly growing. The essence of atom is independent of its existence. Existence is something with which God has endowed atoms. A thing is produced by a combination of atomic acts. Atoms which produce things exist in opposed couples as life and death, motion and rest—and possess particularly no duration.

Nothing is stable among things.[48]

Iqbal criticises ideas which stress that the world is unknowable. In conformity with the Holy Qur'an he identifies three sources of cognition—the inner experience, history and nature.

Knowledge is a combination of reason and experience. Iqbal endorsed the sufi view that it is possible for man to have knowledge of God, the surrounding world, and himself. Iqbal propounded the philosophy of action and reshaped the sufi teachings on the part played by intuition in the process of

46. Bausani, "Iqbal's Philosophy of Religion and the West," in *Crescent and Green*, p. 139.

47. The Ash'arite school also believes in the atomistic theory of the universe according to which the universe consists of *jawahir* (tiny particles).

48. See *Reconstruction*, pp. 68-70.

attaining knowledge and the ideal of a perfect man. The sufi's negative attitude towards reason and rationalistic philosophy was most repugnant to Iqbal. He also completely rejected the sufi doctrine of man's estrangement from the practical world.

There was no justification in the history of religion for the mystics' condemnation of the intellect as the source of cognition, he said.[49] In the *Reconstruction of Religious Thought in Islam*, Iqbal was greatly influenced by the ideas of three notable Muslim thinkers. Shah Waliullah's teachings on the essence and form of religion, Syed Ahmad Khan's "Philosophy of Nature" and Jamal-ud-Din Afghani's thesis of the creative nature of Islam had a profound impression on the intellect of Iqbal.

Shah Waliullah taught that forms of religion, i.e. interpretation of basic dogmas, religious commands relating to specific events can and do differ among various peoples, living at different places under separate conditions of time and space. It follows, therefore, that many topical statements which the Holy Prophet (peace and blessings of Allah be on him) addressed to the Arabs are not meant for Indian Muslims. But monotheism (*Tauhid*) which is the essence of religion, is applicable to all peoples and all eras.

Iqbal approved the view of Shah Waliullah that the law revealed by a prophet is specially related to the habits, ways, and peculiarities of the nation to whom the Prophet is specifically sent.

"The Shariat Values (Ahkam) resulting from this

49. See ibid., p. 78.

application (e.g., rules relating to penalties for crimes) are," Iqbal noted, "in a sense specific to that people ; and since their observance is not an end in itself, they cannot be strictly enforced in the case of future generations."[50]

From this premise Iqbal proceeded to lay stress on the value and importance of *Ijtihad* (enlightened judgment).

There was a school of thought among Muslims in Shah Waliullah's time who held that the decisions that were given on religious questions in the tenth century were final. In other words, the right of independent judgment (*Ijtihad*) stands abolished after the tenth century. Shah Waliullah opposed this viewpoint and supported the revival of the Muslim people's right to *Ijtihad* so that they may be able to separate the *Nass* (authentic text of the Holy Qur'an) and prescriptions of the *Sunnah* concerning *Aam* (common phenomenon) from the *zahir* (literal interpretation) of the Holy Qur'an and the *Sunnah* concerning *Khass* (particular phenomenon).

Without such a demarcation, it is not possible to decide whether this or that religious prescription is applicable to a given set of historical conditions.

Iqbal emphasised that *Ijtihad* should not serve individual but social purpose. Only collective *Ijtihad* could be true *Ijtihad*. Real *Ijtihad*, instead of reflecting the opinion of one man should reflect the opinion of the society and should meet the interest of the society. *Ijtihad*, so defined, becomes an instrument of social development.

50. See ibid., pp. 171-72.

Shah Waliullah felt the necessity for a new orientation in Islam, though living at a period of the crises of Mughul Empire he was not yet able to work out a philosophy of Islam suited to modern conditions.

The man who, by knowledge and experience was fully equipped to accomplish this task and who fully realised the importance and immensity of the task in full measure was Jamal-ud-Din Afghani. [Only] If his indefatigable but divided energy could have devoted itself entirely to Islam as a system of human belief and conduct, the world of Islam, intellectually speaking, would have been on a much more solid ground today."[51]

The diversity of pursuits did not allow Afghani to enunciate an expanded philosophical and political conception of Islam adaptable to modern social conditions.

Sayyid Ahmad Khan, in the opinion of Iqbal, had taken a great step forward in this direction. Sayyid Ahmad Khan propounded a philosophy of Nature according to which the essence of religion lay in the correspondence of religious dogmas to the phenomenon of Nature. Sayyid Ahmad believed that God had imposed an objective causality on Nature. Life exists independently in accordance with the objective laws of Nature.

"This philosophy," thought Iqbal, "offered a new orientation of Islam". Sayyid Ahmad's philosophy was especially attractive for Iqbal, because it recognised that man could know the world, study the laws

51. Ibid., p. 97.

of Nature and utilise them for the development of society.

There was one lacuna in Sayyid Ahmad's thought. He denied the right of man to change the world. Man was so insignificant and unimportant before God that he did not have the strength to bring about new developments in the world. On this point, Iqbal differed sharply with him.

In Iqbal's opinion God had endowed man with the capacity and resources to change the world.

As explained above, Iqbal understood that there was a dialectic movement in nature. This dialectic movement, in his view, extended to society also. Nature, society and man, according to the philosophy of Iqbal, are in constant motion, development and formation. The problem of understanding this dialectic movement in society is a tremendous one as also are the issues confronting the modern generation of Muslims.

"The only course open to us," suggested Iqbal, "is to approach modern knowledge with a respectful but independent attitude and to appreciate the teachings of Islam in the light of that knowledge, even though we may be led to differ from those who have gone before us."[52]

Iqbal's philosophy of the man-activist consisted of two principles. God has endowed man with the ability to create and that there is an inseparable link between human action and society.

This philosophy had already found expression in his first philosophical poem *Asrar-i-Khudi.* Why

52. Ibid., pp. 97-98.

did Muslim society decline in India ? The reason lay in *nafi-i-khudi* (loss of self-consciousness in human personality). The only means of progress among Muslims in India was the regaining of human personality's self-consciousness (*ithbat-i-khudi*).

Against the forces of evil the individual must display firmness, daring and fortitude. Human personality could find perfection and immortality only by waging a victorious struggle against evil.

In *Rumuz-i-Bekhudi*, Iqbal wrote a dialogue between coal and diamond. Between the lines there lies the contrast beween the man who reconciles himself to the slave position (the spineless coal) and the personality seasoned in battle which strives to uproot evil and violence not in the beyond but in the real, earthly world (the diamond which has the glory of light).

The answer to all the questions confronting Muslim society lay in this advice.

> "Be void of fear, grief and anxiety,
> Be hard as a stone, be a diamond."[53]

In *Rumuz-i-Bekhudi* Iqbal taught that vigorous activity for social progress could turn man from a biological individual who is mortal into a personality that acquires immortality.

These concepts of *Asrar-i-Khudi* and *Rumuz-i-Bekhudi* found their final shape in the *Reconstruction of Religious Thought in Islam.*

"The ultimate aim of the ego", said Iqbal, "is not to *see* something, but to *be* something. It is in the ego's effort to *be* something that he [person] discovers his final opportunity to sharpen his objecti-

53. R. A. Nicholson, Tr., *The Secrets of the Self,* p. 106.

vity and acquire a more fundamental 'I am' which finds evidence of its reality not in the Cartesian 'I think' but in the Kantian 'I can'. . . The final act is not an intellectual act, but a vital act which deepens the whole being of the ego, and sharpens his will with the creative assurance that the world is not something to be merely seen or known through concepts, but something to be made and re-made by continuous action."[54]

Iqbal did not share Kant's agnosticism and believed that human action should have no other purpose but to serve God and society.

Iqbal was well aware of the conflict between man and society ; whereas the individual wants to exercise his free-will, the society seeks to subject him to certain restraints.

This conflict, in Iqbal's view, could be resolved only by subordinating self and society to the service of God. God could be served only by following the moral and ethical principles of Islam.

Man is obliged to submit to his Creator, but is not helpless before Him.

God created the universe but He also created free-will and capacity in man to change the universe. In fact, change in this world depended on the dynamic activity of man. Good social activity aims at establishing social justice.

A people or nation must follow the principle of self-help.

There is a constant conflict between Good and Evil.

54. *The Reconstruction*, p. 198.

Human action alone can determine which of these two forces will prevail.

This dialectic philosophy also served to highlight the contrast between the West, whose civilisation, in Iqbal's opinion, was on the road to ruin, and the East, which was awaiting its renovation and seeking its own particular direction of historical progress. The changes in the world situation were the result of inevitable historical progress. While on the subject of historical inevitability Iqbal asserted that only Muslims see in history "the continuous collective movement, a real, inevitable development in time."[55]

Iqbal had a vision of an "ideal Islamic Society" in the modern sense, but did not work out the details of its socio-economic structure. The ideal Islamic Society would be democratic, free from the dominance of an organised priestly class (because Islam has no priesthood) and tolerant towards people professing other faiths.

In this State there shall be no distinction between secular or religious, for *Din-i-Islam* (the Islamic code of life) comprehends both. The temporal as well as religious authority is vested in State. The keynote of this society will be social justice and humaneness. Its supreme guide will be collective *Ijtihad* on Qur'an and *Sunnah*.

Iqbal's socio-political values were essentially religious. The pivot of all his philosophic and political ideas was *Tauhid*. Translated in social terms, the idea of *Tauhid* (belief in one God) meant "equality, solidarity, and freedom".[56]

55. Ibid., p. 14. 56. Ibid., p. 154.

All men are equal before God. Hence all men must have a just and equitable share of economic and social benefits.

In order to attain their objectives Muslims must forge unity among their ranks. Finally, Iqbal desired above all a victory for the Muslims as well as for all the peoples of the East in their struggle for freedom from colonial rule. In his international outlook and opposition to all forms of human oppression such as the exploitation of the East by the capitalist West, of peasants by landlords and of labour by capitalist, Iqbal ranked among the most progressive thinkers in India.

Many of Iqbal's philosophical poems and satirical works reflected that his political sympathies lay with the exploited as against the exploiter and with fighters against oppression rather than with the indifferent and submissive.

Iqbal recognised that the people of the subcontinent were not sufficiently prepared for a mass revolutionary struggle such as had brought victory to the people of the Soviet Union. In the circumstances, he preferred an evolutionary form of progress towards freedom. Expressing his warm regard for Mustafa Kemal as well as approval for his government's right to introduce religious reforms, Iqbal wrote :

> "The truth is that among the Muslim nations of to-day, Turkey alone has shaken off its dogmatic slumber, and attained to self-consciousness."[57]

But at the same time Iqbal openly disagreed with Kemal Ataturk's position on the Caliphate."[58]

57. Ibid., p. 162.

58. See ibid., pp. 154-162.

The conditions in the subcontinent were such that a revolution on Turkish lines was irrelevant. The peoples of the subcontinent, wrote Iqbal, had not yet sighted their own path in the struggle for the creation of an independent State. Internal problems admitted of no easy solutions. He was, however, convinced that self-determination was necessary for the Muslims of India and separate State of their own was their final destiny.

Iqbal had worked on his Lectures on the "Reconstruction of Religious Thought in Islam" for three years. He regarded them as the expression of his mature philosophic and rational interpretation of Islam. He hoped that others would follow him in a responsible *Ijtihad.* Through these Lectures Iqbal wanted to lay down at least for the present age the groundwork for religion and science to "discover hitherto unsuspected mutual harmonies." To Professor Yusuf Salim Chishti. Iqbal confided : "If this book of mine [the Lectures on Reconstruction] had appeared in the reign of Mamun-al-Rashid (Abbasid Caliph 813-833 A.D.), it would have had profound repercussions in the entire intellectual world of Islam."[59]

59. Wahid-ud-Din *Ruzgar-i-Faqir*, vol. I, p. 184.

2

Towards Pakistan

In 1926 Iqbal was elected member of the Punjab Legislative Council. Before understanding the true significance of Iqbal's performance as member of the Punjab Legislative Council, we must take into account the economic and political milieu of the province in that period. The population of the Punjab was composed of Muslims (55%), Hindus (35%), located mostly in districts East of the Ravi, and Sikhs (13%).

The three communities lived in a state of perpetual conflict in almost all walks of life, religious, economic, political, educational and social. In the rural areas the Muslims formed 57% of the population. The Muslims during their rule had treated Muslims and Hindus with even-handed justice. While the Muslims owned most of the agricultural land of the Punjab, the Mughuls allowed the Hindu moneylender a monopoly in trade and finance. The economic position of the two communities was thus balanced. The Sikh rule did not materially change this position either. Both the Mughul and Sikh governments had kept a restraint on the power of the moneylender to extort undue interest from debtors. The main Hindu *bania* (moneylending) castes were Aggarwal, Khatri and Arora. When the British finally wrested Punjab from the Sikhs in 1849, they followed a policy of economic *laissez-faire*. The *bania* was legally and socially freed from all restraints. The British magistracy zealously supported the *bania* in recovering his debts, even allowing him to confiscate the property, house, goods, tools and animals of the defaulting debtor. With the entire weight of the British power thrown on the side of the *bania*, the poor peasant found himself entirely at the mercy of his creditor. In 1870, the province was in the grip of a severe famine. And in this year the *bania* found his golden opportunity to expropriate the houses and lands of the masses. The farmers were so impoverished that they could pay neither debt nor interest. On the other hand, they needed more credit to rehabilitate themselves. Mortgages had been very rare during Mughul or Sikh times, but now mortgages appeared in every village and town of the Punjab. Sir Malcolm Darling[1] gives staggering figures. In 1875-78, the total land area under mortgage was 1,65,000 acres. It almost trebled in 1884-88, during which period 3,85,000 acres of land were under mortgage. In 1868, the number of those engaged in moneylending business was 53,263. Under British patronage this class proliferated and in 1911 they counted 1,93,890. Finally, even the British were frightened of the enormous economic power of the *bania*. S. S. Thorburn investigated the economic situation and published his findings in *Musal-*

1. *The Punjab Peasant* (London, Oxford University Press, 1947) pp. 172-73.

mans and Moneylenders in the Punjab (London, 1886). The British were moved to pass what was called the Land Alienation Act (1900) which came into operation in 1901.

The object of the Act was stated to be the emancipation of peasants from the extortionist economic rule of the moneylender. Under this Act, the non-agricultural classes were debarred from owning land. The owners were forbidden to transfer land to non-agricultural buyers. The non-agriculturalists were legally disqualified to keep the land in mortgage for more than twenty years.

The Act served British interests remarkably well. The peasant proprietor began to look upon the British as his deliverers and he became a staunch supporter of British rule. Political and economic interests were sharply divided into urban and rural thus serving the imperial policy of "Divide and rule". The Act, however, did not eliminate debts. The debts still hung over the peasant like Damocle's sword. The irony was that even farm labourers and tenants who did not own an inch of land were involved in debt. In 1900, the number of families of tenants and agricultural labourers who worked on land but did not own it was 1.25 million. By 1930, they were under a debt liability of Rs. 20 crores.

The land-owning peasants owed to the money-lenders a sum of Rs. 120 crores. The total debt liability of peasant-proprietors, tenants and farmers was thus Rs. 140 crores, out of which the debt of the Muslim peasant-proprietors alone amounted to Rs. 80 crores.[2] Incidentally, the debt of Rs. 140 crores was $26\frac{1}{2}$ times the land revenue extracted by the British administration.

The Act did not affect the landlord class, because they were by and large free of agricultural debt. Though the Punjab on the whole was a province of small peasant-proprietors, yet there were certain districts where as much as 40% of cultivated land was owned by landlords holding more than 50 acres. The area where big Muslim landholdings could be found were Multan, Jhang, Mianwali, Muzuffargarh, Dera Ghazi Khan and Rawalpindi. The Hindu landlords had large holdings east of the Ravi in Rohtak, Hissar, and Ambala. The landlords extracted rents and tributes of several kinds including women from the tillers of the soil, and the British government backed them to the hilt in the recovery of these levies. The peasant worked to the last ounce of his energy to satisfy the demand of the landlords and the British Revenue Officer, yet neither the landlord nor the British administration did anything to raise the quality of rural life by provision of decent wage, mass education, sanitation, medical help etc. The relationship of the landlord and the Government with the tiller of the soil was, therefore, entirely one-sided. Sometimes the landlord assumed the function of a *Pir* (or religious guide) of his tenants and then the exploitation of the tenant knew no bounds. While the money flowed in from rural areas, the landlords lived mostly at Lahore paying court to British officials. They were polygamous, had their sons educated at Aitchison and daughters

2. Ibid., pp. 14-15, 21.

at Queen Mary (both prestigious institutions founded by the British after the manner of English public schools), and generally maintained posh bungalows and *de-luxe* American cars.

From 1880 to 1900 the British were developing the wastelands of Shahpur, Lyallpur (now Faisalabad) and Montgomery (now Sahiwal) districts into fertile tracts by laying out a network of irrigation canals. By this scheme the British sought to accomplish two purposes. First, it increased their revenue income. Second, it gave them an opportunity to oblige loyal rural elements with grants of land. As the British were consolidating their political and economic hold over the countryside a new development was taking shape in cities. In the second half of the nineteenth century, many colleges and universities (under Government or private patronage) were founded all over the subcontinent.

In the Punjab the first batch of graduates from Government College, Lahore passed out in 1870. The University of the Punjab was founded in 1882. Forman Christian College was established in 1864. The Punjab Public Library was set up in 1888. This same period saw the opening of Islamia College in Lahore. Thus in the opening decades of the twentieth century there appeared in towns a sizeable body of well-educated, intelligent, and articulate middle class which was poised to answer the British in their own tongue in legal, constitutional, and economic matters. In their bewilderment the British rapidly began to take counter measures. Titles of Khan Bahadur and Nawab Sahib for Muslims and Rai Bahadur and Rai Sahib for Hindus were liberally conferred on landowning families. These titles were supplemented with land grants in the newly developed canal colonies. This titled and landed aristocracy became the pillar of British Authority in the rural areas and a counterpoise to the rising educated middle class in cities. The British exploited the rural Punjab for revenue for the Government and infantry for the Army. The landlords parasited on the peasantry. Both were frightened of the educated urban middle class who was beginning to grasp the reality of this exploitation and had commenced to voice its protest. This middle class, moreover, had striven to gain political strength by evolving all-India social, educational and political organisations.

The British decided that, in order to preserve the Punjab countryside from the influence of the urban educated class, the province must be kept backward in constitutional reforms. The Punjab was always the last and least favoured province in terms of the introduction of constitutional reforms. Bombay and Madras had their legislative councils in 1861 ; Bengal in 1863 and U. P. in 1866. In the Punjab the Council was established as late as 1897. The Indian Councils Act of 1892 provided an increase in membership of the councils and directed that reserved seats be filled by indirect elections from public and municipal bodies. The provisions were implemented in all provinces save the Punjab. The Council set up in the Punjab in 1897 was restricted to nine members nominated by the Governor. The Punjab had a population of 20 million and Assam only 7 million, yet the two provinces were paired together in the Minto-Morley Scheme (1909).

Under this Scheme both provinces were given a thirty-member legislature each. The Lieutenant Governor of the Punjab had no Executive Council until 1920. The first Punjab Legislative Council under Montagu-Chelmsford Reforms (1919) was constituted in 1921. The Muslims formed an overall majority of 55% in the province, but they were allotted only 50% share in the membership of the legislature. With seven representatives from special constituencies and nominated members, the position of the Muslims was further reduced to that of a minority group which formed only 45% of the Council.[3]

The composition of the Council was as follows :

Elected members = Muslims (35) + Sikhs (15) + Hindus & Others (21) = 71

Nominated Officials & Non-Officials = 23. Total = 94

In 1909, the Minto-Morley Reforms had conceded the principle of separate electorates. It guaranteed that separate constituencies shall be clearly demarcated for every community.

The All-India Muslim League and the Indian National Congress at a joint session in Lucknow in 1916 concluded an agreement on the mode and quantum of communal representation in the Indian Legislative Councils. According to the "Lucknow Pact," as the agreement came to be known, the Muslims accepted the doctrine of weightage.[4] This was a

3. See Azim Hussain, *Fazl-i-Hussain*, pp. 150-53.

4. The doctrine of weightage meant that Muslims would have to forgo a percentage of seats in their majority provinces in return for more representation in those provinces where they were in a minority : 29% in Bihar where their population strength was 13% ; 15% in C.P. which had a Muslim population of 4%. See Ishtiaq Hussain Qureshi, *The Struggle for Pakistan*, (Karachi University Press, 1965), pp. 46-47.

major concession. For example, in Bengal the Muslims agreed to surrender a quarter of the seats in the Legislative Council, to which they would otherwise have been entitled on the basis of their population in the province.

The Congress accepted the principle of separate electorates without reservation. The agreement provided that Muslims would get 35% representation in Bombay where they constituted 20% of the population; 30% in Uttar Pardesh (then United Provinces) where the Muslims stood 14% in the population.

In November 1932, in the elections held under the Montagu-Chelmsford Reforms, Iqbal was persuaded by friends and admirers to stand from a Muslim constituency of Lahore. Iqbal's opponent Malik Muhammad Din campaigned vigorously, but Iqbal rarely went out for canvassing. He won the election by personal prestige among the voters. The constituency had a total of 12,000 registered voters. Sixty-eight per cent of them actually polled their votes. Iqbal obtained 5,675 votes against 2,498 secured by Malik Muhammad Din.[5]

The Legislative Council Iqbal entered was dominated by feudal landlords, who were loyal to the core to their British masters and were staunch

Muslim hopes of gaining anything by the "Lucknow Pact" proved illusory. The system of weightage was in fact, completely artificial. However, true to their realization of national self, the Muslims held firm to the principle of separate electorates. Khaliq-uz-Zumman (*Pathway to Pakistan*, Lahore, Longmans, 1961) and Ashiq Hussain Batalvi (*Iqbal Ke Akhri Do Sal*, pp. 70-75) opine that the "Lucknow Pact" brought to the fore Muslim fears of Hindu domination in the Muslim majority provinces.

5. *The Civil & Military Gazette*, Lahore, 30 Nov. 1932.

conservatives in politics. Yet these gnomes were shrewd enough to be primarily concerned with protecting and enhancing their own vested interests. When their own interest clashed with that of the urban population, they were always ready to trample upon the interest of the latter. Since they themselves lacked political sophistication the landlords were forced to look for a leader from among the elite urban middle class. Their choice proved happy for them. They could not have found a better man than Mian Fazl-i-Hussain, a shrewd political manipulator. Fazl-i-Hussain, a city barrister, was a convinced believer in the *status quo*. He believed that power in the Council must rest with feudalists. The principal object of the National Unionist Party, founded under the leadership of Fazl-i-Hussain, was to uphold the ascendancy of landed interests. The Hindu and Sikh landlords, therefore, found no hesitation in joining the Unionist Party. Outside the precincts of the Assembly the Unionist Party had no existence. It was only a political club of the landed gentry of all communities presided over by Mian Fazl-i-Hussain. The Unionist Party never wanted, nor had, any contacts with the people. Even otherwise, there was a political vacuum in the Punjab of those days. Parties of all-India standing like the Congress and the Muslim League had no effective organisation in the province.

A branch of the Indian National Congress had been established in the Punjab in 1885, but until 1930 it had no mass support even among the Hindus. The Punjab Muslims who supported the Congress never counted more than a handful. The Arya Samaj had been hostile to the Congress since 1889.[6]

The Samaj was partisan to the interests of the Hindu *bania* at the time of the passing of the Land Alienation Act, 1900. Much against the wishes of the Samaj, the Congress did not support the Act because its policy was not to antagonise the peasant-proprietors of the Punjab. As stated earlier, Iqbal's sympathies with Muslim League dated back to his studentship days in London. He desired that the Muslim League should blossom into a truly mass party. However, the Provincial League was no more than a political toy in the hands of two scheming men, Mian Muhammad Shafi and Mian Fazl-i-Hussain. The All-India Muslim League at its Karachi Session (1907) approved Shafi League as its *bona fide* branch in the Punjab. A compromise was effected between Shafi and Fazl-i-Hussain, as a result of which the latter became the League's Joint Secretary. Mian Shafi who remained head of the League till 1916 was ardently supported by Iqbal. Fazl-i-Hussain's heart, however, lay with the Punjab feudalists. Except Iqbal, no Punjab politician had a broad all-India outlook. When Fazl-i-Hussain founded the Unionist Party, his link with the League became formal, even obstructive. In 1926, the Punjab League was a paper organisation. The dominant group in the Legislative Council was the Unionist Party. The urban pro-Hindu Swaraj Party and the Khilafat Party had returned a handful members each. The Opposition consisted of a

6. See Lala Lajpat Rai ; *Autobiographical Writings* (New Delhi 1965), pp. 85-95.

sizeable group of Hindu Sabha.

On his election to the Legislative Council Iqbal faced two alternatives : to join the Unionist Party or to form a separate block of like-minded urban Muslim members. The decision was not easy for Iqbal, but with his characteristic clear-mindedness he found an answer without compromising his cherished principles. The Unionists were an alliance of Muslim and Hindu feudalists.

Their support for the Land Alienation Act and separate electorates for Muslims was assured. If Iqbal and his like-minded urban Muslim members had formed a separate group, the Unionist strength would have been seriously impaired. In this case the Congress and the Hindu Sabha groups, who overtly desired to rescind the Land Alienation Act and the system of joint electorates would have gained the upper hand. Membership of the Unionist Party, therefore, seemed to Iqbal as the lesser of the two evils.

Fazl-i-Hussain's main loyalty was to Muslim landed interests. He wished to serve the Punjab Muslims in so far as their interests did not clash with those of the landed gentry. Iqbal, on the other hand, was consistently loyal to the Muslim League and interests of the Muslim masses and vehemently opposed to the vested interests of the landed gentry. A clash between two men was, therefore, natural and inevitable. Iqbal maintained nominal membership of the Unionist Party during his term of office (1926-30) as member of the Punjab Legislative Council. On every vital question, however, he exasperated Fazl-i-

Hussain and his feudal Unionists by subjecting them to forthright criticism. Especially noteworthy was his criticism of the revenue policy which suited the feudal interests and the educational administration which operated to keep the Muslim masses down in the educational field. The land policy which was in vogue in India of the classical age (c. 300-700 A.D.) was that fallow or waste-land owned by the State was generally given by way of salary to functionaries of the State. The cultivated land, also owned by the State, was treated as Crown land, i.e. providing income for the royal family. In theory this land too could be donated to officers of State in consideration for their services. The third category of land was that which was in private hands and upon it the Government levied various rates of taxes from age to age.[7]

The Muslim rulers, including the Mughuls had adopted the same system with slight amendments. On assumption of rule in the subcontinent the British devised their revenue system on an altogether different basis. The British enunciated the doctrine of the imperial ownership of all land. If a subject occupied land, he was obliged to pay a share of its gross income to the imperial government in return for the protection it afforded him. The British administrators and publicists refined and elaborated this doctrine after Lord Curzon, during his viceroyalty (1899-1905), had assiduously enforced the policy of the Crown's ownership of the entire

7. Romila Thapar, *A History of India* (Baltimore, 1966) I, 46.

land.[8]

The landlords of the Punjab grouped themselves into the Unionist Party, and loyally supported this imperial policy. Speaking in the 1928 spring session of the Legislative Council, the member from Simla, Lala Mohan Lal, endorsed the assessment of the Punjab Revenue Minister, Mian Fazl-i-Hussain, regarding the principle of the Crown's ownership of all agricultural land. The doctrine was vehemently opposed by Iqbal. Proving the fallacy of imperial assumption with reference to history he said that the proposition that all land belonged to the Crown was a barbarous theory. Neither in ancient India, nor even in the days of the Mughuls had the sovereign ever claimed universal ownership of the land. "We are told that the Mughuls claimed such rights; but the people of the Punjab owned and possessed the land of this country long before the race of Babar entered into history, the unmistakeable lesson of which is that crowns come and go; the people alone are immortal. Iqbal thought that the Unionist's support of the imperial revenue policy was a fitting occasion for the application of that humorous Punjabi proverb *Chor nalon pand kali* which by implication meant that the Crown was thief and the Unionists were readier to help the thief than the thief was to help himself. Impartial scholars and historians like Peron (1777) and Briggs (1830) had already proved that the British doctrine of state ownership of the entire land amounted to no more than imperial avarice.

8. W. H. Moreland, *India at the Death of Akbar* (London 1920); *also see* Percival Griffiths, *The British Impact on India* [London, 1965].

Iqbal stated that Briggs particularly gives in his book an accurate description of the laws of Manu, of Muslim law and practices prevailing in various parts of India, Bengal, Malwa, the Punjab, etc. and arrives at the conclusion that in no period in the history of India the State ever claimed the proprietorship of land.

Iqbal declared that the land revenue system was most iniquitous. Since it made no distinction between a small landholder and an absentee landlord, Iqbal recommended that land tax should be converted into a graduated income-tax. The Government did not tax a person who earned Rs. 2,000 per year from sources other than land. Yet it imposed revenue on a peasant-proprietor who earned far less than this sum. This distinction, in Iqbal's view, was another injustice which flowed from the Government's land revenue policy.

It was considered that eight acres was the minimum economically viable unit in the Punjab. On behalf of those small farmers who eked out their living from landholdings of up to five acres, Iqbal pleaded that their land should be exempted from revenue. The suggestion piqued the Revenue Minister Mian Fazl-i-Hussain who immediately pointed out that this exemption would cause a loss of Rs. 2,50,00,000 to the Government Budget. He put the minimum economical landholding at about ten or eleven acres and argued that remission of five acres, as demanded by Iqbal, would provide no relief to the peasantry and would be tantamount to committing a fruitless sin.

Iqbal agreed that by adopting such a measure the Government would incur a loss of Rs. 2½ crores in revenue receipts, but it would show, he told Fazl-i-Hussain, that there is at least some sense of justice in you.

Iqbal's suggestions implied a transition from feudal structure of the society to a more egalitarian set-up. As has been said earlier, his views on land policy presaged future developments.

In his speeches during the 1929-30 sessions Iqbal twice made some provocative suggestions to curb the vested interests of the bureaucracy, which were even bolder than his attacks on feudal interests. The bureaucratic elite, composed mainly of the British, drew enormous salaries, allowances which coupled with spacious housing facilities, servants, furloughs, pensions and gratuities, gave them a much higher standard of living than any other comparable class of bureaucracy in the world. Referring to this, Iqbal categorically stated in the Council : "We spend much more than any other country in the world on the present system of administration. We pay much more than our revenues justify." He informed the House that "there are to my mind only three alternatives open to the people, either have the present system with all its ugly daughters, such as deficit Budgets, communal bickerings, starving millions, debt or unemployment or do away with the present system root and branch, or retain the form of the present system and secure the power to pay less for it. There is no other alternative. This system must come to an end if you want to live a comfortable life."

The statement drew a strong protest from the British officials and Iqbal's suggestion that large cuts be made in the salaries of the bureaucrats was dismissed out of hand.

Nothing daunted Iqbal. He now assailed the combined interest of all the three classes, capitalist, feudal and bureaucratics. He suggested that an inheritance tax be imposed on the inheritors of property to the value of twenty or thirty thousand rupees and described it as "Death Duties".

"Living Duties", Mian Fazl-i-Hussain retorted quickly, "would be more appropriate."

"It is the living who will have to pay", Iqbal declared triumphantly.

Not unexpectedly, the Legislative Council, dominated by the above-mentioned classes, did not adopt Iqbal's proposals. These ideological struggles brought Iqbal to the conclusion that land as a means of production should not be in private ownership, but should be socialised for the benefit of all.[9]

Educationally, the Muslims were the most depressed community in the Punjab. Even on the whole the Punjab was not a very advanced province in education. Until 1920, in a population of twenty million only 2.4% were receiving education. In view of this, speaking on the cut motion on the Government's demand for a grant under "Education", Iqbal pointed out that "the disinterested foreign Government in this country wants to keep the people ignorant".

The British policy of grants-in-aid to schools

9. The idea is expressed in the poem "Al-Ard Lillah" (Land Belong to God), *Bal-i-Jibril*, p. 161, where he says that earth belongs neither to the landlord, nor to him (the poet) ; It is God's.

mainly favoured the moneyed classes ; the Hindus. The Punjab Government's rule was to give more aid to those schools which had already more funds at their disposal. Thus those who spent more received more. The Muslims formed the majority in the province, but the bulk of them were economically depressed. The Muslim educational institutions were consequently poor. According to the rule, "spend more and receive more aid" the Muslim educational institutions received only nominal grants-in-aid from the Government, whereas the Hindu institutions, well-provided already, received substantial grants. No wonder, the Muslim institutions failed to compete with those of the Hindus. In his speech on 4 March 1929 in the Budget session of 1929-30, Iqbal pointed out the injustice of withholding financial help from those educational institutions which needed it most. He gave statistics to highlight the disparity in the treatment meted out to Muslim and non-Muslim institutions.

Iqbal suggested that the Government should distribute funds equally, especially "in places where people are backward and too poor to pay for education".[10]

10. These were the statistics quoted by Iqbal : In 1922-23 fifty-two new schools were granted monetary assistance. Among these only sixteen were Muslim schools. During this year Rs. 29,214 only were granted to Muslim schools out of a total allocation of Rs. 1,21,906. In the fiscal year 1926-27, the total amount of grants-in-aid was Rs. 1,22,287 out of which Muslim schools received Rs. 29,214 only, or 23% of the total. In 1927-28, the Muslim schools were granted Rs. 2,04,330 out of the total allocation of Rs. 10,13,154.

In his speech of 7 March 1930, Iqbal pointed out that grants-in-aid were provided to twenty-one schools in 1928-29. Of these thirteen were Hindu schools, six Sikh, and only two Muslim schools. The Hindu schools received an amount of Rs. 16,973, the Sikh schools were given Rs. 9,908; the Muslim schools were granted a paltry sum of Rs. 2,200.

Actually there were certain political reasons behind this policy of discrimination against the Muslims. The Unionist Muslim members of the Legislature were politically dependent on the support of Hindu members, prominent among whom were Dr Gokal Chand Narang and Manohar Lal, who held the portfolio of Education. An Anglo-Hindu Alliance was also working against the interest of the Muslims. This is borne out by the testimony of Azim Hussain, son of the Unionist Party's leader Fazl-i-Hussain. Azim Hussain reveals that Mahasabha representatives like Manohar Lal and Dr Gokal Chand Narang were kept in office against the wishes of the Unionist Party and that the British Governor used the officially nominated members to give majority to the unpopular minister of Education, Manohar Lal.[11]

This vitiated atmosphere confirmed Iqbal's misgivings about Hindu-Muslim cooperation in a common polity. The period 1922-27 also saw fourteen bloody communal riots between the Hindus, Sikhs and Muslims. On 18 July 1927, Iqbal declared on the floor of the House, "...we are actually living in a state of civil war".[12] On 19 July 1927, he further exposed the fiction of a common nationality in India. "In this country," he stated, "one community is always aiming at the destruction of the other community".[13] Under these circumstances Iqbal wondered if it was desirable to become one nation.[14]

A Sikh member Sardar Ujjal Singh had made a pro-

11. Azim Hussain, op. cit., p. 165.
12. S. A. Vahid, *Thoughts and Reflections of Iqbal*, p. 317.
13. Ibid., p. 322.
14. Ibid., p. 323.

posal in the House to fill Government posts by open competitive examination. Reviewing this proposal Iqbal said in his speech on 19 July 1927 that communication and trust between Hindus and Muslims had broken down. An extreme example of this was the practice adopted in the Punjab University examinations. The University had adopted the system of allotting fictitious roll numbers to candidates in order to conceal the identity of Muslim candidates from Hindu examiners and that of the Hindu examinees from Muslim examiners. However, crafty students managed to reveal their identity by writing religious symbols on their scripts in the hope that their papers might fall into the hands of their co-religionists. Citing his own personal experience, Iqbal narrated : "Only the other day I was reading the LL.B. examination papers. I found the number '786' which is the numerical value of an Arabic formula written on one paper and on others I found 'Om' [Hindu name for God] meant to invoke the blessing of God".[15] Describing another personal experience Iqbal informed the Council that during the riots in Lahore he had accompanied the Muslim deputation to the Deputy Commissioner. The British administration had obviously lost its nerve, for the Deputy Commissioner expressed his inability to control the situation because : "Before the Reforms scheme came into operation, there were 120 British officers in the Police department, but they were only 68 now [in 1927]".[16] The Deputy Commissioner informed the Deputation that both communities wanted European officers in the Police.

15. Ibid., p. 320. 16. Ibid.

Iqbal agreed that honest, impartial British officers were required to control the riots and drew the moral that "the talk of a united nationalism is futile and will perhaps remain so for a long time to come".[17]

Besides these vital questions other interests also claimed the attention of Iqbal. Speaking on the resolution regarding Unani and Ayurvedic system of medicine (22 February 1928) he expressed the opinion that Western medical science had yet to learn much from the Unani system. Many works of Muslim *hakims*, especially those by Najib-ud-Din Samarqandi lay un-published in European libraries. If they were published, they could yet give surprise to those who boast of the superiority of Western medicine. Iqbal demanded Government support for the indigenous systems because they were cheaper in comparison to the European system.[18]

He recommended that an Institute of Pharmacy should be established to teach the *hakims* the improved methods of preparing medicines. At the same time Iqbal thought that the *hakims* should not imitate the Western pharmacopoeia, because our own simple preparations are more natural.

Besides Revenue, Education and Health, Iqbal commented on the then important sphere of Civil administration also. "The small increase in Excise and Stamps revenue is no source of satisfaction, because it means an increase in drunkenness and litigation which reflects credit neither on the people nor on the Government."[19]

Crime, Iqbal thought, was a preventable affair

17. Ibid., p. 321.
18. Ibid., pp. 324-25.
19. Ibid., p. 333.

and demanded that legal eccentricities should be eliminated. The man who stole cattle worth Rs. 10 was sent to jail for two years. Naturally, the prison population would be very large and Government would have to spend huge sums for its upkeep.[20] Iqbal urged that the province should be rapidly industrialised in order to solve the problem of unemployment and bring increasing prosperity to the people. He noted that the Government spent practically nothing on industry. He considered that there was "a good future for weaving industry, and for shoemaking industry in this province."[21]

Iqbal's Assembly Speeches are characterised by a clear grasp of social and economic problems. Their direct and forceful style, flashes of wit and high seriousness of purpose rank them in the class of sublime oratory.

In all-India politics Iqbal consistently endeavoured to establish a separate Muslim political identity.

From the late 1920 began that political interaction between Iqbal and M. A. Jinnah which turned the latter from a sincere believer in Hindu-Muslim cooperation to an inveterate and unflinching champion of an independent destiny for Indian Muslims.

On 20 March, 1927 a "Unity Conference" was held at Delhi at which M. A. Jinnah as President of the League and Srinivasa Iyengar, as President of the Congress, concluded an agreement which came to be known as "Delhi Proposals !"

The two leaders agreed :

(1) To accept a system of joint electorates. provided that

20. Budget Speech, 4 March 1929, reproduced in ibid., p. 334.
21. Budget Speech, 7 March 1929, reproduced in ibid., p. 340.

Sind was separated from the Bombay province and reforms were introduced in the North-West Frontier Province and Baluchistan.

(2) To reserve seats for all communities in all provinces.

(3) That in Bengal and the Punjab (the two predominantly Muslim-majority provinces) the allocation of seats would be in proportion to population. (This clause abrogated the "Lucknow Pact".)

(4) That in the Central Legislature Muslim seats were to be no less than one-third of the total seats.[22]

In retrospect it was a solid achievement to get the Congress agree to the above proposals. The Quaid-i-Azam was accepting joint electorates in exchange for sure safeguards for Muslims in all Provinces.

In the large Muslim-majority provinces of Bengal and Punjab, the allocation of seats would at any rate be in proportion to the population.

The "Delhi Proposals" thus contained the germ of Pakistan.

The All-India Congress Committee "substantially accepted the Muslim proposals" in a resolution passed in May 1927.[23]

In December 1927, sub-committees were appointed both by the League and the Congress to prepare an agreed draft based on the "Delhi Proposals" of the Constitution of a self-governing India.[24]

The Punjab Muslim League, under the leadership of Mian Muhammad Shafi, Mian Fazl-i-Hussain and Iqbal raised a voice of dissent from the "Delhi Proposals"

22. M. H. Saiyid, *Mohammad Ali Jinnah* (Lahore : Ashraf, 1953), pp. 238-39.

23. Rajendra Prasad, *India Divided*, (Bombay, 1947) p. 127.

24. Waheed-uz-Zaman, *Towards Pakistan* (Lahore : 1964), pp. 34-35.

The Congress, too, betrayed the Delhi Agreement by adopting the Nehru Committee Report at the All-Parties Conference (12 February to 15 March 1928). The composition of the Nehru Committee with its parity of Muslim and Hindu Mahasabha members, besides Congress and liberal Hindus is revealing.

It consisted of :

(1) Pandit Motilal Nehru (Chairman)
(2) Ali Imam (Muslim)
(3) Shuaib Qureshi (Muslim)
(4) M. S. Aney (Hindu Mahasabha)
(5) M. R. Jayakar (Hindu Mahasabha)
(6) G. R. Pradhan (Non-Brahmin Hindu)
(7) Sardar Mangal Singh (Sikh League)
(8) Sir Tej Bahadur Sapru (Liberal Hindu)
(9) N. M. Joshi (Labour)

The Nehru Committee recommended separation of Sind from Bombay and the elevation of the North-West Frontier Province and Baluchistan to the status of constitutional provinces, but it did not concede reservation of seats in the Punjab and Bengal. Also, it insisted that the Central Government retain Residuary Powers and that Muslims compose only 25% of the Central Legislature.

The Congress decided that if the British Government did not agree to a Constitution framed along the lines of Nehru Committee Report, by 31 December 1929, they would initiate a policy of non-violent non-cooperation.

Meanwhile the British Government set up the Simon Commission "to make recommendations for future constitutional reforms in India". The Commission visited India from February to March 1928 and again from October 1928 to April 1929. The Commission was violently opposed throughout India. The Muslim League split into two divisions on the question of the attitude to be adopted towards the Commission.

One section of the League had M. A. Jinnah as President and Dr Kitchlew as Secretary. The other was led by Muhammad Shafi (President) and Iqbal (Secretary). The Shafi section of the League met in Lahore (1928). It rejected the "Delhi Proposals" and offered cooperation to the Simon Commission. Meeting in Calcutta (1928) the Jinnah League disowned the Shafi faction, adopted the "Delhi Proposals" and declared its non-cooperation with the Simon Commission. It also proposed the following modifications to the Nehru Committee Report :

(1) Muslim representation in the Central Legislature should not be less than one-third.

(2) In the event that adult suffrage, as proposed in the Nehru Report is granted. the Punjab and Bengal should have seats only on population basis subject to re-examination after ten years.

(3) The Residuary Powers should be vested in the Provinces and not in the Centre.

(4) The separation of Sind from Bombay and raising North-West Frontier Province to the status of a Governor's Province should not be made contingent on the establishment of the constitution framed by the Nehru Committee.[25]

M. A. Jinnah who consistently had two purposes

25. See Rafi Ahmad Kidwai, *Proceedings of the All-Parties National Convention*, Calcutta 1928, *All-Parties National Convention*, Allahbad, 1929, p. 78.

in mind (*a*) safeguard of Muslim rights; and (*b*) joint front with Congress to oust the British, pleaded with the Congress to adopt the League's modifications.

The Congress refusal to do so shook M. A. Jinnah's confidence in that organisation once for all.

The Shafi League convened a meeting in Lahore in May 1928 and proceeded to draft a memorandum for the Simon Commission. Iqbal urged the imperative necessity of provincial autonomy. The meeting adopted a temporary draft for circulation among other leaders of the League for eliciting their views. In the meantime Iqbal went to Delhi for medical treatment and stayed there for a few weeks. In his absence the Shafi League released the draft for publication in the Press. Mian Shafi's conservative attitude appalled Iqbal. He considered it a reactionary approach to Constitutional problems. Accordingly, he resigned his position as Secretary of the Shafi League.

In his letter of resignation, Iqbal told Shafi, "I now find that the extract of the League memorandum as published in the Press makes no demand for full provincial autonomy and suggests a form of Provincial Government in which Law, Order and Justice should be placed under the direct charge of the Governor. This suggestion is only a veiled form of diarchy and means no Constitutional advance at all".[26]

Iqbal's vigorous reaction had the desired effect. Mian Shafi staged a quick somersault and adopted

26. "Shamloo" Ed., *Speeches and Statements of Iqbal*, pp. 163-64.

Iqbal's proposals. Iqbal, thereupon, withdrew his resignation and approved the final draft of the memorandum.

The deputation of the Shafi League waited on the Simon Commission on 5 November 1928. During the course of the interview Iqbal helped Shafi in answering the Commission's queries.

The Muslim leadership, however, soon realised the need of national unity to offer effective counter-measures to the machinations of the Congress and the British Government. The idea of an All-Parties Muslim Conference was initiated by leading Muslims including Iqbal.

The Jinnah League and Shafi League alongwith other Muslims assembled at the All-Party Conference (later designated All India Muslim Conference) in Delhi on 31 December 1928-1 January 1929.

Sir Sultan Muhammad Khan Agha Khan was elected Chairman of the Conference. In view of the Congress claim for "complete independence" put forth at its Lahore session on 31 December 1929, the Muslim Conference strongly demanded the following safeguards for the Muslim community :

> "The future constitution must be federal with maximum of autonomy and the residual powers vested in the province ; that the separate electorate and weightage must be retained ; and the Muslims must have their due share in the Central and Provincial Cabinets".[27]

In 1934, the two Leagues merged and elected Quaid-i-Azam M. A. Jinnah as President.

27. Sir Reginald Coupland, *India, A Restatement* (London : Oxford University Press, 1945), p. 130.

In the period 1930-1934 Iqbal provided the ideological leadership, spearheading the Muslim demand for a separate Muslim State.

A truly Islamic order of life can flourish only under an Islamic State. The socio-political conceptions formulated in the *Reconstruction of Religious Thought in Islam* led Iqbal to the conclusion that the Islamic ideals of social equality, economic justice and freedom from all forms of exploitation could be embodied only in an independent Islamic State. The idea of a separate homeland for the Muslims of India was the logical outgrowth of the reconstruction of Islamic thought. This was most fully reflected in the political speeches, letters and political tracts of the 1930's.

The first necessity in order to win self-determination for Muslims was to prove that Muslims constituted a nation in the subcontinent. Several notable Muslims, prominent among them being Maulana Abul Kalam Azad, tried to differentiate between the concepts of national community (*Qawm*) and religious community (*Millat*). But Iqbal had no doubts on this point. He considered Indian Muslims a nation, *Qawm* and *Millat* combined.

In 1930, at the Allahabad session Iqbal was elected President of the All-India Muslim League.

In his Presidential Address to the Indian National Congress at Lahore in December 1929, Pandit Jawahar Lal Nehru had declared "Purna Sawaraj" (complete independence) as the immediate demand of the Congress. In his 1930 address to the Muslim League at Allahabad, Iqbal put forward the idea of a separate

Sovereign State for Muslims. He declared : "Indeed the Muslims of India are the only people who can fully be described as a nation in the modern sense of the word".

Iqbal emphasised that it was the basic characteristic of the devotees of Islam to consolidate on a religious basis. Under colonial rule, this desire which "to-day is being gradually realised in the countries of Islam and in the shape of what is called Muslim nationalism," gets intensified. This emergence of Muslim nationalism (the consciousness of a national-religious community) substantiated the necessity of State self-determination for the Muslims of India.

"I would like to see", declared Iqbal, "the Punjab, North-West Frontier Province, Sind and Baluchistan amalgamated into a single State. Self-government, within the British Empire or without the British Empire and the formation of a consolidated North-West Indian Muslim state appears to me to be the final destiny of the Muslims, at least of North-West India".[28]

Indian and Western historians and politicians have cast serious doubts on the sincerity of Iqbal in his demand for a separate homeland for Indian Muslims. Pandit Jawahar Lal Nehru says :

> "He (Iqbal) supplied in fine poetry which was written in both Persian and Urdu a philosophic background to the Muslim intelligentsia and this diverted its mind in a separate direction. His popularity was no doubt due to the quality of his poetry, but even more it was due to his having fulfilled a need when the Muslim mind was searching for some anchor to hold on to. The old Pan-Islamic ideal had ceased to have

28. Vahid, op. cit., pp. 170-71.

any meaning ; there was no Khilafat and every Islamic country, Turkey most of all, was intensely nationalist. Nationalism was in fact the dominant force in Asia as elsewhere, and in India the nationalist movement had grown powerful and challenged British rule repeatedly. That nationalism had a strong appeal to the Muslim mind in India, and large number of Muslims had played a leading part in its struggle for freedom. Yet Indian nationalism was dominated by Hindus and had a Hinduised look. So a conflict arose in the Muslim mind. Many [Muslims] began to drift in a separatist direction for which Iqbal's poetic and philosophic approach had prepared them. This I imagine was the background out of which in recent years arose the cry for a division of India".

After admitting that Indian nationalism was Hinduised and that Iqbal had launched the separatist movement, Jawaharlal Nehru says in the same breath :

"Iqbal was one of the early advocates of Pakistan and yet he appears to have realized its inherent danger and absurdity. Edward Thompson had written that in the course of conversation, Iqbal told him that he had advocated Pakistan because of his position as President of the Muslim League session, but he felt sure that it would be injurious to India as a whole and to Muslims especially. Probably he had not given much thought to the question previously, as it had assumed no importance then. His whole outlook on life does not fit in with the subsequent development of the idea of Pakistan or division of India."[29]

Jawahar Lal Nehru could not be expected to have closely followed the evolution of Iqbal's political thought over the years. His knowledge of Iqbal was second-hand. As Iqbal showed in his reply to Nehru's dabbling in the Qadiani question, the Pandit's knowledge of Islam was cursory.

29. Jawaharlal Nehru "Muslim Nationalism," *Discovery of India*, (New York, 1946), p. 353.

In spite of these drawbacks, if Nehru had referred to the text of Iqbal's Presidential Address at Allahabad, he would not have honestly come to the hasty conclusion, nor would he have lent a willing ear to Edward Thompson's apocryphal story.

Iqbal had spelled out the idea of Muslim State in no ambiguous terms. He had defined a nation and indicated its geographical home. He emphasised that "the Muslim demand for the creation of a Muslim India within Indian subcontinent is perfectly justified". It was only after affirming this idea of a separate State that Iqbal referred to a federal scheme for India, basing the formation of autonomous regions on "linguistic and economic community and religious unity".

Jawahar Lal Nehru did not as well imbibe the message of Iqbal's letter in which Iqbal had defined Muslim nationalism as permeated with ideas of social justice clothed in religious form and a religio-political community desirous of forming a State.

Clarifying the nature of conflict between nationalism and Islam, Iqbal wrote to Jawahar Lal Nehru :

"Nationalism in the sense of love of one's country and even readiness to die for its honour is a part of the Muslim's faith ; it comes into conflict with Islam only when it begins to play the role of a political concept and claims to be a principle of human solidarity demanding that Islam should recede to the background of a mere private opinion and cease to be a living factor in the national life".[30]

Having thus demolished the Congress case for a unified secular nationalism, Iqbal proceeded to inform Nehru that nationalism was a problem for

30. "Reply to Questions Raised by Pandit Jawaharlal Nehru," in Vahid, Ed., op. cit., p. 287.

Muslims only in those countries where they were in the minority (such as India): "In majority countries Islam accommodates nationalism for there Islam and nationalism are practically identical".[31]

The address which turned the course of history in India was the apex point of Iqbal's political career. All his previous ideas culminated in this address and all his subsequent actions and those of the Muslim nation were dictated by it. Using identical language M. A. Jinnah in his Presidential Address to the All-India Muslim League session in March 1940 re-stated Iqbal's two-nation theory.

The Congress was, however, loth to consider the two-nation theory and continued to harp on the tune of a common Indian nationality right up to the time of Partition in 1947.

Meanwhile, in 1930 the British Government called a Round Table Conference in London to discuss a Federal Constitution for India with proper safeguards for minorities, States and other interests.

On 12 November 1930, the first session of the Conference opened in London. All Indian political parties were represented, except the Congress whose leaders were in jail. Prominent representatives of the Muslims included Sir Sultan Muhammad Khan Agha Khan, Sir Mian Muhammad Shafi and M. A. Jinnah. The first conference concluded with a consensus that India should have a federal government. There was a widespread feeling, however, that "general agreement had been reached only because of the absence of the Congress Party."[32]

31. Ibid., pp., 287-88.
32. Coupland, op. cit., p. 330.

At the second Round Table Conference (7 September to 1 December 1931), the Congress was represented by Mr. Gandhi alone. The Muslim delegation to this Conference now included Iqbal.

Out of Conference, most discussions between the delegation and Mr. Gandhi took place in the suite of Sir Agha Khan at Ritz Hotel, London. The Agha Khan says: "Always the argument returned to certain basic points of difference: was India a nation or two nations" ?[33]

The Muslim delegation contended that there were profound religious, cultural and racial differences dividing various communities in India. The territorial unity of India had been imposed by the British for administrative reasons. Indian unity as it then existed was artificial and transient. Mr. Gandhi, however, remained obdurate and, in the words of Agha Khan, "this ultimate disagreement on point of principle could not be bridged".[34] In the course of the Conference, Iqbal worked as member of the Committee on Minorities. Here, too Gandhi insulted all the minorities and particularly Muslim delegates by questioning thier representative character and declared that he alone represented all India.[35]

Iqbal issued a statement on 6 December 1933 which throws considerable side-light on his work during the Round Table Conference. Pandit Jawaharlal Nehru in one of his statements had charged the

33. Agha Khan, *Memoirs* (London, 1953), p. 228.
34. Ibid., p. 229.
35. See "Presidential Address of Iqbal, All-India Muslim Conference Lahore, 21 March 1932", in Vahid, Ed., op. cit., p. 198.

Muslim delegates to the Conference with reactionaryism.

Iqbal rebutted the charge and recounted the inner history of the negotiations between the Muslim delegation and Mr. Gandhi :

"Pandit Jawaharlal has described His Highness the Agha Khan as the greatest inspirer of "political reactionaryism" among Muslims. The truth, however, is that it was Agha Khan himself who assured Mr. Gandhi in the presence of several Indian delegates, including myself, that if the Hindus or the Congress agreed to Muslim demands, the entire Muslim community would be ready to serve as his [Mr. Gandhi's] camp followers in the political struggle.

"Mr. Gandhi weighed the Agha Khan's words and his offer to accept Muslim demands came later and was hedged round with conditions. The first condition was that he [Mr. Gandhi] would accept the Muslim demands in his personal capacity and would try to secure, but not guarantee, the acceptance of his position by Congress."

Iqbal asked Mr. Gandhi to wire to the Congress Executive and secure its consent to his offer. Mr. Gandhi merely replied ; "I know the Congress would not make me their plenipotentiary in the question." During this conversation Mrs. Sarojini Naidu, the far-famed poetess of India, was sitting beside Iqbal and the two shared some observations about the attitude of Mr. Gandhi. Iqbal invited Mr. Nehru to confirm the history of these negotiations from her.

Proceeding, Iqbal revealed : "Mr. Gandhi was then asked (by the Muslim delegates) to secure at least the Hindu and Sikh delegates' consent to his offer. He did make something like an attempt to do so but failed and privately expressed his disappointment with their attitude." The second and, in the words of Iqbal, the most unrighteous condition that Mr. Gandhi put forth was that Muslims should not support the special claims of untouchables, particularly their claim to special representation. In reply, Iqbal says : "It was pointed out to him [Mr. Gandhi] that it did not lie in the mouth of Muslims to oppose those very claims on the part of the untouchables which they were advancing for themselves and that if Mr. Gandhi could arrive at a mutual understanding with the untouchables the Muslims would certainly not stand in their way."[35a] Mr. Gandhi, however, insisted on this condition.

Iqbal pointed out to Mr. Nehru that the Agha Khan's offer made in 1931 still held good in 1933. If, however, Mr. Nehru could not persuade the Hindus or the Congress to agree to the safeguards which Muslims believed to be necessary for their protection, then he should at least not accuse Muslims of political reactionaryism, "but leave those who understand the motive and purposes of Hindu Communalism to

35-*a*. It was M. A. Jinnah who made this reply. The Agha Khan in his *Memoirs* (p. 229) gives an identical version of the same incident :

"I opened it [the discussion] by saying to Mahatmaji that, were he now to show himself a real father to India's Muslims, they would respond by helping him to the utmost of their ability in his struggle for India's Independence. Mahatmaji turned to face me. "I cannot in truth say", he observed, "that I have any feeling of paternal love for Muslims. But if you put the matter on grounds of political necessity, I am ready to discuss it in a cooperative spirit. I cannot indulge in any form of sentiment."

With regard to the trend of the discussion, the Agha Khan says :

"The Mahatma sought to impose a first and fundamental condition : that the Muslims should, before they asked for any guarantees for themselves, accept Congress's interpretation of Swaraj—Self-Government—as their goal. To which Mr. Jinnah very rightly answered that, since the Mahatma was not imposing this condition on the other Hindu Members of the various delegations attending the Round Table Conference, why should he impose it on the Muslim ?"

draw the conclusion that he [Mr. Nehru] is in essential agreement with the Mahasabha in the latters' campaign against the Communal Award."

Jahawarlal Nehru had also accused some Muslims of being "definitely anti-national".

To this Iqbal replied : "If by 'nationalism' he means a fusion of the communities in a biological sense, I should personally plead guilty to the charge of anti-nationalism."

"Measured according to Mr. Nehru's standard Mr. Gandhi was the greatest anti-national in India," said Iqbal, "Mr. Gandhi had made it his life-long mission to prevent the fusion of untouchables with other communities and to retain them in the fold of Hinduism without any real fusion even between them and the caste Hindus."

Iqbal agreed that "a man who opposes nationalism in the sense of a fusion of the communities is not necessarily anti-national".

Pandit Nehru had further alleged that Muslims believed in democracy as a religious institution but were afraid of it in practice.

This charge also was forcefully rebutted by Iqbal. "He [Mr. Nehru] overlooks the fact that the communal electorates and other safeguards on which Muslims insist are only intended to prevent eighty million members of a comparatively poor and backward community from being ousted from all real advantages of democracy."

Mr. Nehru had accused His Highness the Agha Khan, Dr. Shafaat Ahmed Khan and Iqbal of telling a gathering of the members of the House of Commons in London that it was impossible to govern India without the British. "It is unfair", said Iqbal, "to cite the impressions of a Press Correspondent instead of an authorised text of the speeches in such an argument. No Indian can believe for a moment that it is impossible to govern India except by British agency."

In conclusion Iqbal felt constrained to put a straight question to Mr. Nehru : "How is India's problem to be solved if the majority community will neither concede the minimum safeguards necessary for the protection of a minority of 80 million people nor accept the award of a third party : but continue to talk of a kind of nationalism which works out only to its own benefit ?" Iqbal was sure that this position can admit of only two alternatives. "Either the Indian majority community will have to accept for itself the permanent position of an agent of British imperialism in the East or the country will have to be redistributed on a basis of religious, historical and cultural affinities so as to do away with the question of electorates and the communal problem in its present form."[36]

Gandhi's intransigence was the main stumbling block in the way of an agreement.

So the minorities, with the exception of the Sikhs, signed an Indian Minorities Pact and gave it to the British Prime Minister. In consultations within the Muslim delegation, Iqbal proposed that the British Government should be advised to accept Provincial Autonomy before the introduction of the

36. Vahid, Ed., op. cit., p. 367.

principle of central responsibility in the Government, of India. In the opinion of Iqbal without the consolidation of Provincial Autonomy a federal constitution could not function in India.

It is not difficult to see Iqbal's reason for laying stress on this particular point. With provincial Autonomy Muslim majority areas in the North-west Zone of India would have become a solid Muslim block checking and balancing the weight of Hindu majority provinces in a federation. The autonomous Muslim majority provinces would also be ready to merge in time in a sovereign Muslim State.

Iqbal's view prevailed in the delegation. On 15 November, the Muslim delegates resolved not to participate in the discussions of the Federal Structure Committee.

In a surprise move, disregarding its earlier decision, the Muslim delegation did participate in the Federal Committee on 26 November and consented to the simultaneous introduction of Provincial Autonomy and central responsibility. Iqbal's comment was that "the Muslim Spokesmen were badly advised by certain English politicians in rejecting the immediate introduction of responsible Government in the provinces of British India".[37]

In protest against this *volte-face*, Iqbal dissociated himself from the delegation.

At the conclusion of the second Round Table Conference, the British Government announced the Communal Award (17 August 1932). The Award gave

37. Percival Griffiths, *The British Impact on India* (London Frank Cass, 1955), p. 330.

separate electorates to the Muslims and other minorities. It also granted the principle of weightage to Muslims in the Hindu majority provinces and to the Sikhs and Hindus in the Punjab.

In practice, however, the Award was actually calculated to reduce Muslim majorities in the Punjab and Bengal into minorities. In the Punjab, for instance, where Muslims constituted 57%, they got only 49% representation ; Hindus with 27% population received 27% seats, and Sikhs forming 13% secured 18% seats in the Legislature. In Bengal the situation was as follows : Muslim population 55% (Seats in the Council 48%) ; Hindu population 43% (Seats 43%).[38]

The Congress attitude to the Award was inconsistent and critical. In a statement explaining the Congress attitude towards the Communal Award issued on 19 June 1934, Iqbal observed :

> "The Congress claims to represent equally all the communities of India and declares that, in view of the sharp difference of opinion in India regarding the Communal Award it can neither accept nor reject it ; yet its comment on the Award amount to a rejection by implication. Consistently with its claim it ought not to have expressed any opinion about the Award."[39]

The Congress Working Committee, in the opinion of Iqbal, had tried by this resolution to hide its inner Communalism. In this vain attempt it had unveiled its designs to such an extent that no Muslim would fail to see through the Congress game.

At this critical juncture, Iqbal advised "the Mus-

38. See I. H. Qureshi, op. cit., p. 64.
39. Vahid, Ed., op. cit., p. 368.

lims of India to stand boldly by the Communal Award even though it does not concede all their demands". He said, as a practical nation, the Muslims had no choice but to adopt this course.[40]

Before the Communal Award was published, Iqbal returned to Lahore (20 December 1931). Iqbal rejected the 1935 Constitution because of its federal provisions. This Constitution had in no way changed the colonial situation in India, and Iqbal berated those who praised the Government of India Act, 1945.

Swim with the tide, flatter their Excellencies
Of the new dispensation that commences !
Would it be more veracious, or—polite,
I wonder, to call an owl the falcon of the night'?[41]

India was a caged bird. The Act of 1935 did not release it. It only sought to comfort it in its bondage. The constitutional reform was a mere eye-wash :

Now he drops withered flowers in our cage, as though
To reconcile his jailbirds to their jail.[42]

In the 'thirties Iqbal's enunciation of the ideal of freedom and active life was perhaps clearer than ever before. Freedom was the basic condition for personal and national development. In the absence of freedom, human capability for goodness is dwarfed. Only the free man has the courage to act and seek the truth. The slave is reduced to lethargy and ignorance.

The thought of a free man is illuminated by Truth ;
The thought of the captive is enslaved to absurdity ;
The subjugated are deluded by wonders of *Pirs*,

40. Ibid.
41. Kiernan, *Poems from Iqbal*, p. 70.
42. Ibid., p. 78 (*Darb-i-Kalim*, p. 64).

While a free man is a living miracle in himself ![43]

To become accustomed to slavery was the greatest misfortune that could befall a man. India was sold out to Britain and her population was a lifeless corpse removed from its grave.

Your fate, poor helpless India, there's no telling
Always the brightest jewel in someone's crown ;
Your peasant a carcass spewed up from the graves,
Whose coffin is mouldering still beneath the sod.
Mortgaged to the alien, soul and body too,
Alas—the dweller vanished with the dwelling—, Enslaved
to Britain you have kissed the rod :
It is not Britain I reproach, but you.[44]

In 1935 a delegation of the Turkish Red Cross visited Lahore. At this time Iqbal wrote "Ghulamon ki Nimaz" (Prayer of the Slaves), depicting in allegorical form the incapacity of slaves for Independent and creative action.[45]

The delegates joined the people of Lahore in prayer at the Badshahi Masjid. The prayer was prolonged. The *Sajdah* (prostration), and recitation lasted a very long time. Talking to Iqbal, the head of the delegation expressed his surprise at the needless prolongation of prayer.

Commenting on this incident, Iqbal wrote :

"The Turkish warrior for the faith said to me after prayer,
Why are your Imams so tedious in the service ?
The simple warrior for the faith and free worshipper,
Did not understand the prayer of the enslaved.
Free people have a thousand tasks to perform,
Their longing for activity gives the law to the nations.

43. *Darb-i-Kalim*, p. 77.
44. Kiernan, op., cit., p. 76.
45. Yusuf Salim Chishti, *Sharh-Darb-i-Kalim*, p. 470.

The body of the enslaved is deprived of the ardour of activity.
For him days follow nights unbrokenly.
What is there strange about the service being tedious ?
What have the slaves to do when they are not at the service ?[46]

Iqbal looked forward to more constitutional reforms in the aftermath of the London Round Table Conferences. He wanted Muslims to organise themselves in order to take full advantage of them. The Indian National Congress and several militant Hindu parties were vociferously decrying the Communal Award and especially its provision for separate electorates. The occasion called for a reinforcement of Muslim solidarity and Iqbal rose to the occasion well. The All-India Muslim Conference held its annual session in Lahore on 21 March 1932 and elected Iqbal as President.

In his Presidential Address to the Conference Iqbal reminded the Muslims to fortify their *Khudi* and offered them several practical suggestions. He said, "Concentrate your whole ego on yourself alone, and ripen your clay into real manhood if you wish to see your aspirations realized".

He advised the Muslims, "Be hard, and work hard. This is the whole secret of individual and collective life. Our ideal is well defined. It is to win in the coming Constitution a position for Islam which may bring her opportunities to fulfil her destiny in this country".

The measures taken for the realization of this ideal "should be partly political, partly cultural".

46. *Darb-i-Kalim*, p. 162.

In the first place, Muslims should evolve "one political organization with provincial and district branches all over the country".

This party should be open-minded, "to make it possible for any school of political thought to come into power, and to guide the community according to its own ideas and methods". This would make division in Muslim ranks impossible and would also "reintegrate and discipline our scattered forces to the best interests of Islam in India".

In order to build up a strong Muslim party Iqbal asked the Muslims to subscribe to a fund of "50 lakhs of rupees".

Iqbal also envisaged "the formation of youth leagues and well-equipped volunteer corps throughout the country under the control and guidance of the Central organisation".

The youth leagues should actively concern themselves with social service, cultural reform and commercial organisation of the Muslims. This latter aspect, *i.e.* the economic organisation and uplift of the Muslims and peasants was always uppermost in Iqbal's mind.

The Muslim peasants were so heavily indebted to Hindu moneylenders that in the words of Iqbal they "had reached the breaking point as in China in 1925, when peasant leagues came into being." Iqbal therefore advised that "Muslim agriculturists cannot be allowed to wait for the drastic remedies provided by agrarian upheavals".

"The future of Islam in India", said Iqbal, "largely depends on the freedom of Muslim peasants in the Punjab".

It was, therefore, the duty of the youth leagues to help "the peasantry in escaping from its present bondage".

As regards the cultural problems, Iqbal suggested the founding of male and female cultural institutes in all the big towns of India". Those institutes should have nothing to do with politics and should make the younger generation aware of "what Islam has already achieved and what it has still to achieve in the religious and cultural history of mankind"

The cultural institutes were further advised to maintain close academic relationship with old and new Muslim educational centres "to secure the ultimate convergence of all the lines of our educational endeavour on a single purpose"

Finally, Iqbal suggested that "an assembly of *ulama* which must include Muslim lawyers who have received education in modern jurisprudence" should be created.[47] This body was, "to protect, expand and, if necessary, to reinterpret the laws of Islam in the light of modern conditions".

Iqbal recommended that this assembly of *ulama* should be accorded a legally recognized position.

"No bill affecting the personal law of Muslims may be put on the legislative anvil before it has passed through the crucible of this assembly".[48]

47. The creation of such a body of *ulama* was announced by the Government of Pakistan in April, 1977. During the first Constituent Assembly of Pakistan, a proposal for the creation of the Ulama Board was adopted. These organisations, at least in idea, owe their existence to Iqbal's suggestions of 1932.

48. Vahid, op. cit., pp. 215-19.

From 1932 to the last day of his life in 1938 Iqbal zealously devoted himself to the reorganisation of Muslim League as a mass political party in the Punjab.

In this endeavour he was bound to come into conflict with the power clique in the Punjab which was composed of Muslim and Hindu feudal gentry led by Fazl-i-Husain and, after his death in 1936 by his successor, Sir Sikandar Hayat Khan. The British Government's decision to hold elections in the provinces during January, February 1937, gave rise to feverish political activity. In May 1936, the League resolved to nominate a Parliamentary Board. The Board was entrusted with the task of drafting a platform and organising election campaign in the provinces.

In the early months of 1936 the Punjab political scene was dominated by two stalwarts, Fazl-i-Husain and Iqbal. After serving the Viceroy as his Executive Councillor Fazl-i-Husain had returned to the Punjab to infuse new life into the Unionist Party.

He was busy in collecting into one party big Muslim, Hindu and Sikh landlords and urban capitalist interests.

Iqbal, on the other hand, was endeavouring to convert the Muslim League into a mass political party.

M. A. Jinnah arrived in Lahore in May 1936 in connection with the organisational work of the League. Iqbal at this time impressed on him the necessity of deriving strength from the support of the common man.

The objective, though laudable, was a long-term one. The elections were near and the League's organisation was almost non-existent. Faced with this dilemma, M. A. Jinnah sought to convert political leaders of the Punjab and urged Fazl-i-Husain to accept the discipline of the League's Parliamentary Board.

Rather than give a straightforward reply Fazl-i-Husain indulged in constitutional hair-splitting. He argued that Provincial autonomy meant decentralisation; therefore, it was wrong to admit central control over provincial elections. Since conditions in each province varied it was impossible to follow a uniform principle.

In the Punjab it was impossible to secure a Muslim majority through separate control of elections. Finally, in many provinces Muslims might find it necessary to have non-communal organisations, and in that case a central Muslim agency was obviously out of the question. Fazl-i-Husain preached to the Muslim League to show "elasticity and initiative" to gain political support of Hindu landlords and moneylenders. He declared in an abusive tone that "Elasticity and initiative should not be sacrificed for the sake of an all-India leader's aspiration".[49]

Mr. Jinnah suggessted that Fazl-i-Husain and the Muslim members of the Unionist Party could form alliances with other groups inside the Assembly according to the usual democratic practice, but they should stand at elections as League candidates. Fazl-i-Husain had contended that in many provinces

49. *The Civil and Military Gazette*, Lahore, 7 June 1936.

Muslims might find it necessary to have non-communal organisations. Referring to this M. A. Jinnah replied : "Why, the Congress is more progressive and non-communal than the Unionist Party. Why not join the Congress Party ?"

M. A. Jinnah called on Iqbal at his Mecleod Road residence. No longer in good physical health, Iqbal was yet content in spirit to see the Muslim League progressing towards his ideal under the leadership o: Muhammad Ali Jinnah, the man whom he had whole heartedly accepted as his leader. On 8th May, 1936, Iqbal, Khalifah Shujauddin, Malik Barkat Ali and their supporters issued a statement in which they stated : "Our nation has full confidence in Jinnah's integrity and political judgment. It is for this reason that now the reactionary leaders are flustered. Jinnah's organisational endeavours would shatter illusory leadership of the selfish leaders, because the Muslims would now elect their true representatives in the forthcoming elections."[50] On 12th May 1936, at a special meeting of the Punjab Muslim League in Lahore the following office bearers were elected. President, Dr. Shaikh Muhammad Iqbal; Vice-Presidents, Malik Barkat Ali and Khalifa Shuja-ud-Din, Secretary, Ghulam Rasul Khan ; Joint Secretaries, Mian Abdul Majid and Ashiq Husain Batalvi. The meeting pledged support to the Central Parliamentary Board and its policies. Even the Majlis-i-Ahrar and Ittihad-i-Millat buried their differences over the Shahid Ganj Mosque and joined forces with the Punjab Muslim League. On

50. Ibid., 9 May 1936 ; Ashiq Husain Batalvi, *Iqbal Ke Akhri Do Saal*, pp. 312-13.

21 May the Quaid-i-Azam announced the membership of the Central Parliamentary Board. Iqbal's name ranked first in this list. Out of the total quota of eleven members from the Punjab, three seats were allocated to Ittihad-i-Millat and four to Ahrar, reserving only four seats for the Punjab Muslim League. Thus the Central Parliamentary Board showed ample appreciation of the cooperation offered by the Ahrar and Ittihad. The Ittihad group presided over by Maulana Zafar Ali Khan seceded from the compact on the pretext that it had not been given parity with Ahrar. The Ahrar too broke away. Both parties later opposed the League at the elections.

After the death of Fazl-i-Husain on 9 July 1936, Sir Sikandar Hayat Khan became the boss of the Unionist Party. At about this time a prominent and influential Unionist, Malik Zaman Mehdi Khan, joined the Muslim League. The Malik was an able man and a sagacious organiser. Iqbal welcomed his conversion and co-opted him as Vice-President of the Punjab Muslim League. On the recommendation of Iqbal, the Malik was also included in the Parliamentary Board.

Iqbal now proceeded to organise the election campaign. He appointed two committees to popularise the League message in the Punjab :

(1) The Draft Committee for drawing up the League Platform. Members : Khalifa Shuja-ud-Din, Syed Tasaddaq Husain, Shaikh Mohammad Husain, Muhammad Azim Khan, Malik Barkat Ali, Malik Zaman Mehdi Khan, Ghulam Rasul Khan, Ashiq Husain Batalvi and Muzaffar Ali Khan Qazilbash.

(2) *The Propaganda Committee.* Its members were younger men like Raja Ghazanfar Ali Khan, Pir Taj-ud-Din and Mian Muhammad Shafi, Secretary of the Punjab Muslim Students Federation.[51]

At Iqbal's invitation the Quaid-i-Azam again arrived in Lahore on 9 October 1936 to inaugurate the League's election campaign. The Punjab League had no uniformed Volunteer Corps at that time. At last the volunteers of the Anjuman-i-Islamia, Amritsar, were mustered and they presented a smart guard of honour to their leader at the Railway Station. The Quaid-i-Azam passed two weeks in Lahore, discussing, advising and generally overseeing the League preparations for elections.

On 11 October, the Punjab Muslim League held a public meeting outside Delhi Gate, Lahore. Iqbal was scheduled to preside over this meeting but was prevented by illness to do so. In this place Malik Zaman Mehdi Khan chaired the meeting. The Quaid-i-Azam was the principal speaker. Addressing the audience he severely criticised the Unionist Party for serving vested interests and for being interested only in fortune hunting. The Quaid-i-Azam's forthright utterances gained him vast popularity among the masses and helped to build up the prestige of the Muslim League. However, the Unionists had two overwhelming factors in their favour, the feudal *Baradari* system and money, which returned them to power. After all the Muslim League had been riddled with factionalism and had only recently been united. It did not have much time before the elec-

51. Batalvi, op. cit., pp. 312-13.

tions to bring its message home to the masses.

The overall result of 1936 election in India is an interesting eye-opener, because it shows the communal character of the Congress. The total seats in all Provincial Assemblies were 1585, out of which the Congress won 711. This sounds impressive. But careful analysis will reveal that the six provinces in which the Congress won a clear majority were Hindu majority provinces, *viz.* Madras, United Provinces, the Central Provinces, Behar, Orissa and Bombay. In Muslim majority provinces the Congress suffered a humiliating defeat. In Bengal, it won only 60 seats out of 250, in the Punjab 18 out of 175 and in Sindh 8 out of 60, and the places where it won were all Hindu constituencies. As for Congress Muslims they contested 58 seats and returned to only 26.

The composition of the Punjab Legislative Assembly was as follows: Unionists (89)+Congress (18)+Non League Muslims (4)+Muslim League (1) +Akali Party (10) + Khalsa Nationalists (13) + Non-Congress Sikhs (13) + Independents (27)= Total =175. Sir Sikandar Hayat Kan formed the Ministry by forging a coalition between the Unionists, the Khalsa National Party and the Hindu Election Board Party.

Elated at their victory the Unionists determined to suppress the rise of Muslim League in the Punjab. The Congress, humiliated at their poor showing, started a "Mass-contact movement to wean the Muslims away from communal parties." Pandit Jawaharlal Nehru was the moving spirit behind this campaign.

In the Punjab the Muslim mass contact movement of the Congress created an intriguing situation. The Unionist Party found itself in great quandary. The Party would dissolve if the Hindu and Sikh members defected to Congress. In the event of Muslims deserting to Congress, the Unionist Party would equally be annihilated. At this hour of peril, the Unionist Party had no choice but to woo the Muslim League. The motives of the Unionists, however, were hypocritical. Their plan was to offer cooperation to Muslim League on the all-India front. They would forge an alliance with the Punjab Muslim League taking care to appoint their own men to its important offices. They would thus maintain their own political dominance while professing allegiance to the League. Of this policy of the Unionists Iqbal was an inveterate foe. On 11 August 1937, Iqbal reported to the Quaid-i-Azam, "the enthusiasm for the League is rapidly increasing in the Punjab, and I have no doubt that the holding of the session in Lahore will be a turning point in the history of the League and an important step towards mass-contact."[52]

A session in Lahore, as Iqbal had said, was indeed going to be a turning point in the history of the League and of the nation but that was not to be until 1940.

In 1937, the All-India Muslim League Working Committee decided to hold its session in Lucknow (15 October 1937). Sir Sikandar Hayat Khan was given the benefit of the doubt and was invited to

52. *Letters of Iqbal to Jinnah* (Lahore, 1956), p. 25.

attend the session. Iqbal could not attend due to ill health. In the suite of the Quaid-i-Azam on the evening of 16 October was concluded that covenant which later came to be known as "Jinnah-Sikandar Pact." Malik Barkat Ali, Muslim League M.L.A. from the Punjab, was present during negotiations. He asked Sikandar Hayat Khan to assert to the following declaration : "The Unionist Party which had been reorganised by Sir Fazl-i-Husain in April 1936 and which subsequently contested the election of 1937 has ceased to exist ; and the Muslim members of this party, after pledging to the membership, have become members of the Muslim League."[53]

Accusing Malik Barkat Ali of intending to annihilate the Unionists, Sir Sikandar rejected the declaration outright. A warm discussion ensued. Eventually the following four-point declaration was agreed upon :

(1) Sir Sikandar on returning to the Punjab will call a meeting of his party and advise all members of his party who have not already signed the League pledge to do so and join the League. As such they shall be governed by the rules and regulations of the Central and Provincial Boards of the All-India Muslim League. This, however, will not affect the present parliamentary coalition of the Unionist Party.

(2) After the adoption of this arrangement, in all future elections and bye-elections for the Legislature the groups constituting the present Unionist Party

53. Batalvi, op. cit., p. 486.

will jointly support candidates put up by their respective groups.

(3) Muslim members of the Legislature, who are elected on League ticket or accept the League ticket will constitute the Muslim League Assembly Party. The Muslim League Assembly Party shall be free to maintain or enter into a coalition or alliance with any other party consistently with the fundamental principles of the policy and programme of the League. Such alliances may be evolved before or after the elections.

(4) In view of the aforesaid arrangement, the Provincial League Parliamentary .Board shall be reconstituted.

The Premier of Bengal, Moulvi Fazal-ul-Haq, and the Premier of Assam, Sir Saadullah, also pledged support to the All-India Muslim League at the Lucknow Session.

When Sir Sikandar returned to the Punjab, the Unionist Party began to issue incongruous interpretations of the so-called "Jinnah-Sikandar Pact."

Iqbal, President of the Punjab Muslim League, and his prominent colleagues believed that the Unionist Party had merged itself in the Muslim League and no longer existed as an independent party. At the least it was the parliamentary colleague of the League. Hence Sikandar Hayat Khan and his followers must submit to directives of the Punjab Muslim League and its President.

The Unionists fought shy of this interpretation. They looked upon the Lucknow Pact as an expedient and a feat of cleverness on the part of Sir Sikandar.

They averred that by his declaration Sir Sikandar meant only to make the Muslim League an ally of the feudal power structure in the Punjab. Finally, they insisted that their Party existed as an independent organisation and they would not submit to League's control.

The treacherous stand of the Unionists provoked a fierce political battle between Iqbal and Sikandar Hayat Khan, which lasted till Iqbal's demise in April 1938.

Iqbal demanded that Sikandar Hayat should make good his promises given at Lucknow. Sikandar Hayat refused to sign even the ordinary membership form of the League. Inconsistently, he demanded that Unionist Party should have a majority on the League's Parliamentary Board.

To counteract the feudal Unionist perfidy Iqbal, the man of the people, launched in full steam a mass contact movement in the Punjab. Under his direction political workers spread throughout the length and breadth of the Punjab. Within a short period of time, thirty-four branch offices of the Muslim League were opened in rural areas.

Sikandar Hayat retaliated by organising the Punjab Zamindara League. This party pretended to be the guardian of the interests of the Punjabi peasants. In fact, it was designed to protect the interests of the guardian class. Sikandar Hayat Khan moved to attack on another front also. He demanded that the League's finances should be handed over to his party men. It was the decided opinion of Iqbal that Sikandar and his Unionist colleagues wanted to kill the League in the Punjab.[54]

Sikandar Hayat Khan even stooped to offer a deliberate insult to Iqbal's self-respect. In a message to the Iqbal Day function of Punjab Muslim Students' Federation, Sikandar Hayat said : "I propose that in the cities where Iqbal Day is celebrated, the citizens should collect money and present it to the great poet. The Iqbal Committee should immediately open an Iqbal Day Account in the Imperial Bank of India, and his followers and admirers should directly make contributions to this fund."[55]

Iqbal smarted under the suggestion, but kept his composure and came out with a suggestion, which, if implemented, would have revived interest in the political and economic teachings of Islam. In a sublimely worded rejoinder to Sikandar Hayat, Iqbal said : "I feel that the needs of the people as a whole are far more pressing than the needs of a private individual, even though his work may have been a source of inspiration to most people. The individual and his needs pass away ; the people and their needs remain. If the people want to honour me they should establish a Chair for Islamic Research on modern lines in the Islamia College, Lahore." This was the real need of the people. The Unionist exploitation, the landlord *pirs*, were sucking the blood of the masses because nowhere in India has the ignorance of Islamic history, theology, jurisprudence, and sufism been successfully exploited as in the Punjab."

54. *Letters of Iqbal to Jinnah*, letter dated 10 November 1937.
55. *The Civil and Military Gazette Lahore*, 5 Dec. 1937.

Iqbal hoped that his suggestion "will meet the Punjab Premier's approval and his influence will make this proposal a success. I offer a humble contribution of one hundred rupees to the fund."[56]

Such proposals as were calculated to serve the interest of the Muslim people were anathema to the feudalists. Sikandar Hayat Khan, who had all the power and resources to implement this scheme, turned a deaf ear to it. The Unionist chief made yet another move to strangle the Muslim League. The Party was starving for funds and well-to-do people had promised, largely out of personal respect for Iqbal, to make generous contributions to its funds. Sikandar Hayat Khan made such a high-handed display of his official power that many intending contributors backed out of their promises. Iqbal's health had been steadily failing for the past few years and now he felt no longer able to shoulder the onerous responsibilities of office. His titanic struggle against the feudalists had apparently ended in a stalemate, but in reality had engendered a movement of revolt against the Unionist power among the masses of the Punjab.

This movement later culminated in the overthrow of the Unionist clique in 1946 general elections.

On the retirement of Iqbal the Nawab of Mamdot succeeded him as President of the Punjab Muslim League. Unfortunately, at this time the Punjab League fell prey to bickerings and rivalries. Moreover, the question of the Provincial League's affiliation with All-India Muslim League provoked a

56. "Shamloo," Ed., *Speeches and Statements of Iqbal*, pp. 219-20.

great storm.

At the Calcutta Session (17-19 April 1938) the All-India Muslim League rejected the Punjab Muslim League's application for affiliation, whereupon Ashiq Husain Batalvi engaged in a verbal clash with Liaquat Ali Khan, General Secretary of the All-India Muslim League.[57]

After the restraining hand of Iqbal had been lifted, the Punjab Muslim League lost cohesion. The general policy of the All-India Muslim League seems to have been to win over the Unionist Muslims and, therefore, Sikandar Hayat was given every encouragement and was even included in the committee formed to reorganise the Muslim League in the Punjab. But as Iqbal had always warned, subsequent events once again proved the treachery of the Unionists. On 21 April 1938, Iqbal expired. Two years later Pakistan Resolution was passed in Lahore (March 1940). Sikandar Hayat Khan died in December 1942. In the course of his historic speech supporting the Pakistan Resolution, the Quaid-i-Azam forcefully advocated the two-nation theory of Iqbal. The wording of the Resolution itself echoed the language of Iqbal's speech at Allahabad in 1930. The Muslim League now wholly embraced Iqbal's programme of mass contact and became truly a party of the people. Muslim streets in the cities and villages of India resounded with Iqbal's verses, chanted by Muslim League workers. From platform and pulpit, at street corner meetings and in the mosque congregation sermons, Iqbal's message of

57. Batalvi, op. cit., p. 640.

national self-determination was repeated verbatim. "Le Kae Rahain Gae Pakistan" (we shall win Pakistan at any cost) became the universal creed of the Indian Muslims from Khyber to Cape Camorin. The verse and chapter of Iqbal galvanised the masses and the Muslim League won a decisive victory at the 1946 elections.

With the establishment of Pakistan on 14 August 1947, the mission of Iqbal's life was posthumously completed.

3

Call to War

(Darb-i-Kalim and International Questions)

In May 1936, Iqbal published *Darb-i-Kalim* ("The Rod of Moses"), the only poetic collection exclusively devoted to topical, political and social themes. It was sub-titled *I'lan-i-Jang Dawr-i-Hadir Ke Khilaf* (Declaration of War against the Present Era). *Darb-i-Kalim* consists of nearly two thousand verses and is divided into six parts with the following captions:

"Islam and Muslims", "Education and upbringing" "Woman", "Literature and Fine Arts", "Politics of East and West" and a bouquet of twenty poems collected under the title, "The Thoughts of Mehrab Gul Afghan". The whole Book is inspired by Iqbal's everlasting theme, the philosophy of *Khudi* and its development, as well as the need for an active and creative life in accord with the message of the Quran.

In December 1929, at Lahore the Indian National Congress had declared "Purna Swaraj" (Complete Independence) as its aim. To the Muslim League at its Allahbad Session in 1930, Iqbal gave the message of an independent Muslim homeland in India. These currents of thought stirred a massive political activity in the subcontinent in mid-thirtees.

The intelligentsia had become keenly aware of the close bond between Capitalism and Imperialism.

The havoc that the West had already caused in the East and its immoral diplomacy in the contemporary world made profound impression on Iqbal. On 18 August 1936 the Fascist Italy attacked Abyssinia (Ethiopia). The European countries (the so-called Democracies) adopted dilatory tactics regarding the invasion of Abyssinia. They invoked only insignificant economic sanctions against Italy in the League of Nations. Even this measure was not prompted by the noble motive of helping the victim, but was an attempt to defend particular interests in Abyssinia. The Western European Democracies preferred to temporise until Fascist Italy had humiliated defenceless Abyssinia in order to share in the spoils. In *Pass Chih Bayad Kard Ay Aqwam-i-Sharq* ("What is to be Done, O Nations of the East") pp. 58-59. Iqbal had exhorted the Indian Muslims not to place any reliance upon member countries of the League of Nations, because they were only "coffin thieves".

"Fate brings incessant struggle,
From the plight of Abyssinia, we must draw a lesson,
Europe placidly and without hinderance
Allows wolves to devour lambs.
There must be a new order in the world.
A solution cannot be anticipated from coffin thieves."

The policy of gaining new colonies and markets was the main cause of fight among Western countries. The spoliation of Eastern nations by the Colonial West was the recurrent theme of Iqbal's poetry in the 'thirtees.

In 1934, he drew attention to the exploitative aspects of European civilisation in the following verses :

One nation feeds on another,
One nation sows the grain and another harvests it.
The lesson of philosophy is to pilfer bread from the hand of the weak.
And rent his soul from his body.
Exploitation of fellow man is the law of the new civilization,
Which conceals itself in the veil of commerce.[1]

In the poem "Abyssinia" in *Darb-i-Kalim* Iqbal prophesied that the European nations' struggle over new markets and new groupings in the world will unleash a second World War. Abyssinia was a corpse which European nations wished to divide as carrion-crows do their spoil.

Little do the European vultures knew
How poisonous is the Abyssinian corpse.
This old carcass is going to disintegrate.
When civilisation is at zenith, minds are bankrupt of nobility.
Nations of the world act like free-booters.
Each wolf seeks an innocent lamb.[2]

From the Vatican, which propagated messages of universal peace and love, the Pope issued no condemnation of the Italian invasion by Abyssinia.

"Alas ! Rome has publically shattered
The holy image of the Church,
O Pope, it breaks the heart that this could have taken place !"[3]

On learning of the economic sanctions invoked against Italy by the League of Nations, Iqbal wrote a poem "Mussolini" in which he indicated that

1. *Pass Chih Bayad Kard Ay Aqwam-i-Sharq*, p. 38.
2. *Darb-i-Kalim*, p. 147.
3. "Abyssinia" in ibid.

parliamentary democracies of the West and Fascism have a common aim, namely, to suck the blood of the people of Asia and Africa.

England, France, Holland and Belgium had extorted great wealth from their colonies. The Italian dictator was merely following their traditions. Mussolini was even better than those colonial powers because he declared his goals openly and did not conceal them under the guise of moral principles like democracy or civilisation.

> Is the crime of Mussolini unique in the world ?
> Exasperation ill befits the European innocents.
> You condemn my longings for Empire.
> Have you not shattered the goblets of weak nations ? . . .
> Mercilessly you have despoiled the tents of the nomads.
> The lands of the peasantry you plundered,
> And pilfered thrones and crowns.
> On the pretext of spreading civilisation,
> You pillaged and murdered yesterday, I do the same today.[4]

As international tensions grew worse, Iqbal saw the clouds of a second World War looming on the horizon. Italy and Germany had set out on a feverish armaments race.

In Asia, Iqbal noted that Japan's design to capture Manchuria which would bring her nearer the border of the Soviet Union was the main cause of her intervention in China. He saw that Imperialist States were busy manufacturing arms to spill blood everywhere in the world. Iqbal condemned each outrage committed by them.

> "To do away with war it is necessary to educate him,
> (the leader of Europe)

4. Ibid., pp. 151-52.

Whose blood-thirsty talons endanger the world.
Europe is engaged in armaments.
Her purpope is to protect false splendour and might."[5]

Evil must be uprooted by *Jihad* (armed struggle). Resignation and pacifism against evil were the worst crimes. The expansion of the Imperialist States must be opposed with armed action.

"We ask the Shaikh, most solicitous about the Church,
If War is evil in the East is it not also evil in the West ?
If you are concerned with truth, then, is it proper
To criticise Islam, and ignore Europe ?[6]

Iqbal pointed out that Empires are founded on the flesh and bones of innocent people. In the poem "Ayk Bahri Qazzaq Awr Sikandar" ("A Pirate and Alexander), he gives a dialogue between Alexander and a pirate. Alexander seizes a pirate and ponders over a suitable punishment for his crimes. The pirate, however, points out that Alexander and he belong to the same trade :

Tyrants both,
Robbers are we, you work on the land and I on the sea.[7]

Governments formed on brute power do not last long.

Alexander stormed like lightning,
And we all know that suddenly he died.[8]

The colonial policy of all Imperialistic States had one common feature. They assumed the role of reformers out to civilise the "barbarous" people of Asia and Africa. Under this pretext they were zealously keeping up the economic supremacy of the West over the East.

5. Ibid., p. 22.
6. Ibid., p. 23.
7. Ibid., p. 157.
8. Ibid., p. 168.

The civilisation that the colonial powers wanted to introduce among the subject races consisted of gambling, drinking and debauchery. Where a guardian of civilisation is needed the issue, today, is not difficult to resolve. The answer is that where there are no dice or women in tight fitting dresses, where it is held an offence to drink wine, there civilisation is needed. The situation in the Middle East claimed Iqbal's most solicitous attention. In his poems he slated the British policy of domination in the Middle East.

The British had brought Syria, Iraq, Palestine and Arabia under their rule by the Treaty of Sevres (20 August 1920). They had promised the Arabs that after eliminating Turkish rule, Arab lands would be modernised.[9]

By 'liberating' Arabia from Turkish rule, the colonialist Britain wanted to establish her own hegemony in that area.

Iqbal strongly objected to the creation of Israel. The British wanted to establish a Jewish State in Palestine because Jews had lived there during the course of history. On that analogy, Iqbal pointed out, the Arabs had an equally good claim to Spain, since their ancestors had ruled there for several centuries, Iqbal clearly saw that the aim of the Jewish State would be to divide the Arabs. Israel would be a serious obstacle to Islam's progress in the world.

> If the Jews have a right to the land of Palestine,
> Why have not Arabs a right to Spain ?

9. Ibid., p. 161.

The aim of British Imperialism (in the Middle East) is not
what it seems.
It is not a question of oranges, honey or dates.[10]

Iqbal knew that the Imperialists adopted different methods with different classes and men in order to break their resistance and bend their opinions to serve imperialist goals. In his belief, Islam was the only guarantee against social abuse and a protection against bondage.

The Imperialists knew that Islam was their principal opponent.

In the poem "Iblis Ka Farman Apnay Siyasiy Farzandon Kay Nam" ("Injunction of the Devil to his Political Offspring"), the devil advises the leaders of colonial countries that they should eliminate Islam from the lands that they wish to subdue, banish the love of Muhammad from the hearts of his followers and inculcate in them respect for European values. How did the Afghans resist colonial expansion? Because they were imbued with the teachings of the Qur'an and had never known slavery.

The man who famine-racked still fears death
Muhammad's spirit from his breast expel!
With Frankish daydreams fill Arabia's brain
Islam from Yemen and Hejaz expel! . . .
Tear from the true believers their traditions
From Khutan's meadows the musk-deer expel!
Iqbal's breath fans the poppy into flame
Such minstrels from the flower-garden expel![11]

Though not opposed to democracy as a system of rule by the consent of people, Iqbal believed that

10. Ibid., p. 159.
11. Ibid., p. 148. Eng. trans. by V. Kiernan, *Poems from Iqbal* (1958), p. 74.

parliamentary democracy of the Western type was a cloak for all forms of exploitation.

> The demon of exploitation dances in the garb of republicanism,
> And you imagine that it is a nymph of freedom.
> Institutions, reforms, privileges and rights.
> Are the Saccharin soporifics of Western medicine.[12]

Democracy often employs gimmicks. Influence and propaganda draw votes and issues are decided by majority of votes. Reason, merit and ability are sacrificed in this process.

> Democracy is a certain form of Government
> In which men are counted but not weighed.[13]

In the philosophical system of Iqbal, "individuality" and "personality" are two distinct entities. "Individuality" is a material fact which democracy "counts" but it does not "weigh" the spiritual fact which is "personality".

Iqbal's satire on Democracy has given rise to the misconception that for Iqbal the rule of one wise man was better than an assembly of asses and that he, like Nietzsche, condemned the rule of the plebeians.[14]

Iqbal himself has denied this charge while explaining the principles of Islamic democracy.

> "Nietzsche . . abhors 'the rule of the herd' and, hopeless of the plebeian, he bases all higher culture on the cultivation and growth of an Aristocracy of Supermen. But is the plebeian so absolutely hopeless ? The Democracy of Islam did not grow out of the extension of economic opportunity, it is a spiritual principle based on the assumption that every human being is a centre of latent power, the possibilities of which

12. *Bang-i-Dara*, p. 261. 13. *Darb-i-Kalim*, p. 150.

14. Kayshap "Sir Mohammad Iqbal and Frederick Nietzsche," *Islamic Quarterly*, II, I, 1955 p. 185.

can be developed by cultivating a certain type of character. Out of the plebeian material Islam has formed men of the noblest type of life and power. Is not, then, the Democracy of Early Islam an experimental refutation of the ideas of Nietzsche ?"[15]

Iqbal outlined the two basic principles of an Islamic Constitution as follows :

"(1) The law of God is absolutely supreme. Authority, except as an interpreter of the law, has no place in the social structure of Islam. Islam has a horror of personal authority. We regard it as inimical to the unfoldment of human individuality. . . ."

"(2) The absolute equality of all the members of the community".[16]

Clearly then, Iqbal was not opposed to rights of the individual, as some critics seem to think. The idea that the individuals' truest self achieves fulfilment in the community alone is to be met with in all his works. The community is like an ocean and the individual, "like a drop which, seeking to expand, becomes an Ocean."[17]

The individual learns discipline through his interaction with his fellow men. Society gives security and preserves the individual. But the individual passes away ; the society and its needs live on. Important though the individual is, he must subordinate his interests to social good and social solidarity. Explaining the relation of individual to society in the ideology of Islam, Iqbal wrote :

When it is said that the interests of Islam are superior to those of the Muslim, it is meant that the interests of the individual as a unit are subordinate to the interests of the

15. S. A. Vahid, Ed., *Thoughts and Reflections of Iqbal*, pp. 83-84.
16. Ibid., pp. 52-53.
17. A. J. Arberry, Tr., *Myteries of Selflessness*, p. 5.

community as an external symbol of the Islamic principle. This is the only principle which limits the liberty of the individual, who is otherwise absolutely free."[18]

To understand the real import of the above passage one must keep in mind the philosophical distinction Iqbal sets up between "individuality" (the material and physical fact) and "personality" (the spiritual fact). Only the "individual" is subordinate to society.

As regards the personality, there is nothing above it except God. Society exists for each person and is subordinate to it.[19]

As can be clearly seen now Iqbal's political philosophy is not unsystematised. It is a well-ordered system based on the political and moral doctrines of Islam.

Turning to world affairs, it is to be noted that Iqbal was one of the first to welcome the Bolshevik Revolution in Russia.[20]

He was sympatethic to worldwide socialist movement and regarded it as "a storm that sweeps away all the foul airs in the atmosphere".

In the opinion of Dr Khalifa Abdul Hakim, Iqbal's attitude towards Socialism was determined by the following factors :

"The *laissez faire* capitalism of the Industrial West had pulverised humanity into hostile national groups, and within every nation too there was class war because the classes of haves and have-nots were at loggerheads. [His Iqbal's] country was predominantly an agricultural country where no industrial

18. Vahid, Ed., op. cit., p. 51.

19. Houben, *The Individual in Democracy and Iqbal's Conception of Khudi*, p. 157.

20. Prof. Aleem Janov, *Pakistan Times*, Lahore, 4 Jan. 1977.

proletariat had developed, but the conflict of the landlord and tenant was becoming an acute socio-economic problem. The usurious moneylender was even more callous than the landlord. Through usury and judicial support of the system set up by the British in complete disregard of local traditions, the ownership of land was rapidly passing into the hands of money-lending owners who did nothing to improve the soil or the condition of the tiller. Iqbal would welcome a revolution in which the do-nothing absentee landlord, or the usurious moneylender, is swept away".[21]

Iqbal had an intense dislike for all forms of injustice and despotism. Economic exploitation had starved and depraved the body. Religious exploitation had shackled the spirit.

His opinion of the capitalist system is best demonstrated in the following verses :

What they call commerce is a game of dice.
For one, profit, for millions swooping death.
There science, philosophy, scholarship, Government.
Preach man's quality and drink man's blood.[22]

In the poem "Ishtirakiat" in *Darb-i-Kalim*, he expressed the idea that socialist revolution in Russia followed the principles of Islam :

"From the behaviour of the nations it appears ;
That the rapid progress of Russia is not without gain. . . .
The truth that lay hidden in the words, "Qul Al-Afw"
May become manifest in this era."[23]

Iqbal invokes in the spirit of Marx and Lenin in *Darb-i-Kalim* to condemn the capitalist exploiters of the West. In the poem "Karl Marx Ki Awaz" ("The Voice of Karl Marx"), Marx exposes the dis-

21. Khalifa Abdul Hakim : *Islam and Communism* pp. 136, 150.
22. 'Lenin Khuda Ke Hadhur Mein', Kiernan, *Poems from Iqbal* (1955) pp. 42-43.
23. *Darb-i-Kalim*, p. 138.

honesty of the European economist who wilfully conceals the predatory nature of Capitalism. They have exploited science to serve as hand-maiden in their game of loot.

> You chessmatch of research and erudition
> You comedy of debate and disputation !
> The world has no more patience left to watch
> This comedy of threadbare speculation.
> What, after all, Sapient Economists,
> Is to be found in your biblification ?
> A comedy of nicely flowing curves.
> A sort of Barmecidal invitation,
> In the idolatrous shrines of the Occident,
> Its pulpits and its seats of education,
> Greed and its murderous crimes are masked under,
> Your knavish comedy of Cerebration.[24]

Iqbal demanded the return of the pristine socialism of Islam. He did not want the atheistic doctrine of Marx or Lenin, but the exploitation free egalitarian economic system of Islam. The basic assumptions of modern socialistic theory, in Iqbal's opinion, was in conformity with Islam.

Atheism, then, was the chief flaw in the socialistic order of Russia. The Soviet anti-religion was a reaction to the depravity and corruption of Roman Catholic Church. But there yet was hope for Russia. Iqbal believed that the Soviet system could not remain Godless for long.

To Sir Francis Younghusband he wrote : "The present negative state of Russian mind will not last indefinitely, for no system of society can rest on an atheistic basis."[25]

24. *Darb-i-Kalim*, p. 139. Eng. trans. by Kiernan, op. cit., p. 70.
25. "Shamloo," Ed., *Speeches and Statement of Iqbal*, p. 167.

M. D. Taseer says that for Iqbal "Bolshevism plus God is almost identical to Islam."[26]

There was no dichotomy between spiritual and material aspects of life in Iqbal's philosophy. Islam comprehends both material and spiritual aspects of life, but, contrary to Marxism, it gives primacy to spiritual.

In the poem "Bolshevik Rus" ("Bolshevik Russia") he declared :

> Those who assumed that the protection of the Church
> Would bring salvation to them
> Were predestined to be the instruments of the destruction of the Church.
> Russian atheism was inspired from on high
> To disrupt the old heathen idols of the churchmen.[27]

The Revolution Iqbal looked forward to would be God-inspired. It would not be wholly materialistic like the Marxist or wholly mystic like the Eastern philosophy, but truly Islamic in character combining both material and spiritual advance. Such a revolution, Iqbal believed, was already at hand.

> A happy life exists neither in Europe nor in Asia,
> There the heart is stifled to death, here the self.
> Within the hearts an impassioned revolution is born.
> The death of the old world perhaps approaches.[28]

Of all the front-rank Muslim political leaders in the twentieth century Iqbal was the only one who interpreted the home and international events in economic terms. On 28 May 1937, he wrote to the Quaid-i-Azam M. A. Jinnah pointing out that the economic plight of the Muslims had been steadily

26. In Introduction to Kiernan, op. cit., (1947), pp. 14-15.
27. *Darb-i-Kalim*, p. 143.
28. Ibid., p. 139.

worsening for the last two hundred years. The Muslims believed that they had been reduced to poverty by the economic exploitation of Hindu money-lenders and capitalists. They did not realise yet that Imperialism was equally responsible for their economic distress. The Muslim League's ultimate success, Iqbal warned, lay in its ability to solve the Muslim's economic problems.

In the struggle between the capitalist and the worker, Iqbal is unmistakably and vehemently on the side of the worker.

Even God commands the Angels :

> Arise ! Wake up the poor of My World,
> Shake the foundations of the palaces of the rich. . . .
> Burn every bushel of corn in the farm-land,
> From which the peasant gets no meal.[29]

In the mid-twenties a new class of industrial workers arose in the subcontinent and an ideology of the working class became a live factor in politics. In 1933, the Communist Party of India was founded. It was proclaimed illegal in July 1934. At the same time the influence of socialist ideas permeated by degrees the young intellectuals, and a progressive movement in literature developed. Iqbal belonged neither to the Communist Party of India nor to the Progressive Writers' Association. He, however, had condemned the theory of "Art for Art's Sake" from the outset of his creative career.

"For Iqbal, language is only the means of expressing his thought. What he really emphasizes is the content. For him the best form was that which

29. *Bal-i-Jibril*, p.147.

could best express the content."[30]

As regards the content, Iqbal brought into his poetical works new themes and subject-matters. The tradition of Urdu literature had been to present erotic themes. He opposed this tradition on the ground that it encouraged low instincts, destroyed spiritual values and harmed national interest. The artists and writers who followed the erotic tradition were condemned by Iqbal in the poem 'Hunerwaran-i-Hind'.

> Their fancy kills love and ecstasy,
> In their dark realms of thought are the sepulchres of nations.
> In their temples they carve symbols of death,
> The Art of such Brahmins is disgusted with life.
> They obscure lofty goals from man's view ;
> They put the spirit to sleep ; and awaken the body
> Woman dominates nerves of the poor Indian poet, painter and the story writer.[31]

Poetry, Iqbal believed, should encourage man to perform noble deeds, spur him to activity and call him to battle against falsehood. From the writer and the artist, Iqbal demanded originality.

> How common has the death of imagination here become !
> The Indian as well as the Persian imitates the European.
> I deplore that the contemporary Bihzad.
> Has lost the eternal joy of the East.[32]

He wanted didactic art and purposeful literature committed to the social, economic and moral ideals of Islam.

In the 'thirties Central Asia was in the melting

30. Ali Sardar Jafri, *Taraqqi Pasand Adab* (Progressive Literature) (Aligarh, 1951), p. 114.

31. *Darb-i-Kalim*, p. 128.

32. Ibid., p. 123.

pot. The Muslim population in Chinese Turkistan was seething with discontent. On 16 May 1933, Iqbal issued a statement on the Rebellion in Chinese Turkistan. He analysed the geo-political causes and economic forces working behind the upheaval. The turmoil started in 1914 when Chinese magistrates were appointed in the area and the Chinese Government made an attempt to impose the Chinese language on the population which was almost wholly Muslim. In 1930, the leader of the revolution was a seventeen year old Muslim boy named Chong Yng. Regarding this precocious General Iqbal related a heart-lifting story that he had heard at a lecture meeting of the Central Asian Society in England in 1932. A certain Mr Petro, member of a European expedition to Central Asia was the guest lecturer. He told his audience that the Muslim General had besieged a Chinese force in the city of Hami.

The Muslim General sent Mr Petro as his personal envoy to the Chinese General to negotiate peace with the besieged Chinese forces. Describing his encounter with the Chinese General, Mr. Petro said :

"I was received by the Chinese General and the Chinese Defence Consul in the city. I was expecting to be questioned regarding the strength and plans of the army of besiegers. Much to my surpirse, however, the first and only question put to me by the Chinese General was : "Is it true that Ma Chong Yng is only twenty years old ?" On being told that Ma was less than that age, the Chinese General turned to the Defence Consul who was in favour of surrendering city and said, "I am eighty-one years old and my hair has been white for a long time. My great-grandson is older than this suckling. How do you think I can surrender this city to an infant?"

The exploits of this "infant" Muslim General which could form the subject of a modern *Odyssey* inspired Iqbal to observe that "the home of Changez, Taimur and Babar has not ceased to produce military geniuses of the highest order".[33]

The main causes of the Turkistan Rebellion, according to Iqbal, were neither religious nor racial, but economic. As regards the race problem, Iqbal believed it to be "an attitude of mind" which he considered to be the greatest blot on modern civilization."[34] Iqbal apprehended "that the birth of a race-problem in Asia will lead to most disastrous results."[35]

Islam is the only antidote to racialism.

> "The main endeavour of Islam as a religion has been to solve this very problem and if modern Asia wishes to avoid the fate of Europe there is no other remedy but to assimilate the ideals of Islam and to think not in terms of race but in terms of mankind."

Iqbal thought that the revolution in Chinese Turkestan might develop into a Pan-Turanian movement. This was something which was dreaded in both Iran and Afghanistan. In any case the revolution in Chinese Turkestan, if it succeeded, was "bound to produce repercussions in Afghan and Russian Turkestan, particularly in the latter which is already seething with discontent owing to religious persecution and owing to serious food problem created in that country by the Russian Government's policy of turning it into a huge cotton farm."[36]

Iqbal had an intellectual and emotional sympathy

33. Vahid, Ed., op. cit., p. 53.
34. Ibid.
35. Ibid.
36. Ibid., pp. 353-54.

with this revolution spearheaded by a seventeen year old Muslim General (evocative of Muhammad b. Qasim). This revolution by the people of Islam was welcome for another very weighty reason. "The success of the revolution will mean the birth of a prosperous and strong Muslim State in Chinese Turkestan where Muslims, who are about 99 per cent of the population, will be freed from the age-old Chinese oppression. Chinese Turkestan is an extremely fertile country, but owing to Chinese oppression and misrule only five per cent of its land is at present under cultivation. The establishment of another Muslim State between India and Russia will push the menace of the atheistic materialism of Bolshevism farther away from the borders of our country, even if it does not drive this menace away from central Asia as a whole."[37]

In 1931 the World Muslim Congress, Jerusalem, elected him member of the various Sub-Committees formed to discuss distinct proposals. In one Sub-Committee he strongly opposed the idea of establishing at Jerusalem a University on the old and antiquated lines of the Jamiah Azhar in Cairo and insisted on the proposed University being of a thoroughly modern type. This gave rise to the rumour that Iqbal was opposed to the setting up of any kind of University at Jerusalem. Reuter circulated the rumour world-wide. Iqbal, therefore, categorically stated :

"I am a strong advocate of Arabic-speaking countries setting up not one but several universities for the purpose of

37. Ibid., pp. 354-55.

transferring modern knowledge to Arabic which is the only non-European language that has kept pace with the progress of thought in modern times."[38]

During his trip to Jerusalem, Iqbal visited the holy places common to Islam, Christianity and Judaism. Christ's birth-place affected him deeply. But what he saw inside the church at Bethlehem was disgusting, because "the Church was divided into three parts which were allotted to the Armenian, Greek and Catholic churches, respectively. These sects continuously fight among themselves, sometimes indulging in bloodshed and defiling one another's altar", and ennobling, because "it is two Muslim policemen who keep the peace among them."[39]

In a statement on the conditions prevailing in Europe issued on 26 February 1933 he said :

"After visiting different European countries and seeing the general moral chaos of the modern world, I am convinced that the great opportunity for Islam as a faith has come."[40]

In Europe he saw a great craving for the knowledge of Islam. The European Muslims were holding a social and cultural conference in Geneva in August of 1933 and Iqbal hoped that Asian and African Muslims will generously respond to the call of the promoters of this conference.

During his 1932 European visit Iqbal visited Cordova, Granada, Seville, Toledo and Madrid and saw the mosque of Cordova[41] and the Alhambra in

38. Ibid., p. 345.
39. Ibid., p. 344.
40. Ibid., p. 350.
41. The mosque at Cordova inspired the famous poem "Masjid-i-Qurtaba."

Granada.

He went to see Madinat-uz-Zahra, the famous palace built on a mountain by Abdur Rahman I for his wife, Zahra. It was there, he recalled, that the first demonstration of a flying machine was given in the twelfth century by a Muslim inventor.[42]

In Spain, Iqbal had a meeting with the Education Minister whom he found to be "an exceedingly courteous gentleman with a breadth of vision hardly to be expected in a country like Spain". He was equally delighted to make the acquaintance of Professor Asin, the well-known author of *Islam and the Divine Comedy*. Iqbal noted with satisfaction that under the direction of the Education Minister the department of Arabic in the University of Granada was being greatly expanded. Iqbal gathered that the movement of reform started by Luther was still "working quietly in different European countries and the hold of priesthood, especially in Spain, was gradually loosening."[43]

In 1933 Iqbal was invited along with others by the Afghan Government to advise on matters connected with the proposed University at Kabul. Iqbal's assessment of the situation was "that younger generation of Afghans are thoroughly in earnest about modern knowledge, and its coordination with their religion and culture."[44]

The Afghans were a fine people and Iqbal considered it a duty to help them advance as much as they could. In this regard Iqbal categorically stated

42. Vahid, Ed., op. cit., p. 350.
43. Ibid., pp. 350-51.
44. Ibid., p. 361.

that he was not recommending a completely secularised system of education for Afghanistan.

"Personally I believe that complete secularisation of education has not produced good results anywhere especially in Muslim lands. Nor is there any absolute system of education. Each country has its own needs and its educational problems must be discussed and solved in the light of those needs."[45]

Giving his impressions of the visit he said in a statement on 6 November 1933 that the first thing he and his colleagues noticed was complete safety of life and property in the country. This he considered a remarkable achievement for a Government which overcame a widespread rebellion only four years previously. The Ministers of the Government were discharging their duties in right earnest. The Government enjoyed the solid backing of the orthodox party. Consequently as a leading divine put it to Iqbal, there was no difference between the Mullas and the young men in Afghanistan.

The Afghan Government proposed to reorganise the entire department of Public Instruction on modern lines and at the same time to improve all roads which connected Afghanistan with neighbouring countries. To begin with two faculties, medicine and civil engineering, were organised at the University. A well-planned road joining Kabul with Peshawar was scheduled to be completed in two years and another road leading to the Russian frontiers had already been completed. This latter road was of obvious strategic importance as it brought

45. Ibid., pp. 361-62.

Central Asia nearer to Central Europe. In an interview with the King of Afghanistan Iqbal gathered that the ruler's sole desire was to see his country flourishing and living in peace and amity with its neighbours".[46]

Iqbal's over-all impression was that "Afghanistan represents today a united country where in every direction one sees signs of a new awakening and where the authorities are engaged in drawing up programmes of well planned work."[47]

In a statement read at a public meeting held under the auspices of the Punjab Muslim League on 27 July 1937, Iqbal expressed deep concern on the injustice done to the Arabs in Palestine.

He condemned the Report of the British Government recommending the partition of Palestine. He exhorted the Muslims of the world to declare that the problem which the British statesmen were tackling was not one of Palestine only, but seriously affected the entire Muslim world.[48]

Studied in its historical perspective, Palestine, said Iqbal, was purely a Muslim problem. More than 1300 years ago, long before Caliph Umar entered Jerusalem, Palestine had ceased to be a Jewish problem. The Jews as Professor Hockings' researches show, had dispersed from the country quite voluntarily and their Scriptures for the most part were written outside Palestine.

Palestine was never a Christian problem either. In the light of modern research it is doubtful that Peter

46. Ibid., p. 362.
47. Ibid.
48. Ibid., p. 369.

the Hermit ever existed. If Crusades were an attempt to turn Palestine into a Christian problem, then this attempt was defeated by the victories of Sultan Salahuddin. Palestine, Iqbal asserted, was therefore a purely Muslim problem.

The idea of a national home for the Jews as enunciated in the Report of the Royal Commission was only a device. In fact, British Imperialism sought a home for itself in the form of a permanent mandate in the religious home of the Muslims. It was a dangerous experiment which betokened serious difficulties for British Imperialism. "The offer of a piece of rich land to the Jews and the rocky desert plus cash to the Arabs is no political wisdom".[49]

Iqbal pointed out that the ruling classes in England were clearly betraying the honour of the British race. "It is a low transaction unworthy and damaging to the honour of a great people in whose name definite promises of liberty and confederation were given to the Arabs."[50]

Iqbal warned that there were important lessons in recent history which the Muslims of Asia ought to take to heart. These lessons were : Firstly, the union of Arabs with Turks. "Experience has made it abundantly clear that the political integrity of the peoples of the Near East lies in the immediate reunion of the Turks and the Arabs. The policy of isolating the Turks from the rest of the Muslim world is still in action. We hear now and then that Turks are repudiating Islam. A greater lie was never told. Only those who have no idea of the history of the

49. Ibid. p. 370. 50. Ibid.

concepts of Islamic jurisprudence fall an easy prey to this sort of mischievous propaganda."[51]

Iqbal urged the Arabs never to forget the consequences arising out of their deserting the Turks in their hour of trial.

The second lesson for the Muslims of the Near East was that they should not depend upon the counsel of the Arab kings who were Agents of Imperialism.

"The Arab people must further remember that they cannot afford to rely on the advice of those Arab kings who are not in a position to arrive at an independent judgment in the matter of Palestine with an independent conscience. Whatever they decide they should decide on their own initiative after a full understanding of the problem before them."[52]

Thirdly, the Muslims must dissociate themselves from the International Body, the League of Nations, and form their own Eastern League of Nations.

"The present moment is also a moment of trial for the Muslim statesmen of the free non-Arab Muslim Countries of Asia. Since the abolition of the Caliphate this is the first serious international problem of both a religious and political nature, which historical forces are compelling them to face. The possibilities of the Palestine problem may eventually compel them seriously to consider their position as members of that Anglo-French institution miscalled the League of Nations and to explore practical means for the formation of an Eastern League

51. Ibid., p. 371.
52. Ibid., pp. 371-372.

of Nations."[53]

In his last public message broadcast as "New Year's Message" from the Lahore Radio Station on 1 January 1938, Iqbal surveyed the contemporary world, diagnosed its ills and prescribed a remedy. "The modern age", he said, "justly prides itself on its vast knowledge and scientific progress." In this age while time and space are being annihilated, he noted with regret that "the tyranny of imperialism still struts abroad, covering its face under the masks of Democracy. Nationalism, Communism, Fascism and heaven knows what else besides. Under these masks, in every corner of the earth, the spirit of freedom and the dignity of man are being trampled underfoot in a way to which not even the darkest period of human history presents a parallel."[54]

Looking back on the year 1937 he saw that in Abyssinia or Palestine, Spain or China, the same misery prevailed in every corner of man's earthly home, and hundreds of thousands of men were being butchered mercilessly.

The people of Spain, though they belonged to one race, one religion, one nation and spoke the same language, were cutting one another's throats and destroying their culture and civilisation by their own hands owing to a difference in their economic creed. This one event showed that national unity was not a durable force.[55]

In this age of self-destruction man's survival de-

53. Ibid., p. 373.

54. Ibid.

55. Vahid Ed., op. cit. pp. 374-75. This is clearly refutation of the one-Nation theory of the Indian National Congress.

pended only on one measure viz. wholesome respect by man of mankind.

"Remember", said Iqbal, "man can be maintained on this earth only by honouring mankind, and this world will remain a battle-ground of ferocious beasts of prey unless and until the educational forces of the whole world are directed to inculcating in man respect for mankind."[56]

Peace will not reign in the world, and man will never be able to lead a happy and contented life and the beautiful ideals of liberty, equality and fraternity will never materialise "so long as this so-called democracy, this accursed nationalism and this degraded imperialism are not shattered, so long as men do not demonstrate by their actions that whole world is the family of God, so long as distinctions of race, colour and geographical[57] nationalities are not wiped out completely."[58]

56. Ibid.
57. Not religious.
58. Vahid, Ed., op cit., p. 375.

4

Iqbal's View of Indian History

(*And His Place in It*)

In 1913 appeared *Tarikh-i-Hind*, a school text-book on the history of India prepared jointly by Dr. Shaikh Muhammad Iqbal M.A., Ph.D. Barrister-at-Law, and Lala Ram Parshad M.A., Professor of History, Government College, Lahore.

In the Preface to the book the joint authors indicate their preference for genuine and authentic history. They believe that a history book should provide sufficient material for the reader to form an independent judgment on events. History, in their opinion, should be written in easy and interesting style and the book should read like a captivating story. The authors are thus inclined towards that class of Historiography which seeks to present to the reader true, authentic and comprehensive material and aims to entertain and instruct him. The following is the verbatim translation of the Preface :

> We have taken scrupulous care to present only the most authentic historical events. The causes of events have also been related and material has been provided for the students to reflect and arrive at independent judgments. Notice has been taken of the success or failure of certain aspects of the British administration. No views, however, have been express-

ed on controversial matters. Our endeavour has been to present to the student the pageant of Indian history in common language and in an interesting style, neither stuffing it with obscure events nor with elaborate detail, so that the students might read it with relish and acquire correct knowledge of history.

The book has been well planned and in its style and language lives up to the claims of the authors. The history of India has been recounted period wise and political, cultural and literary landmarks of each period have been described. The condition of India before and after the advent of the British has been compared and although value judgments have been avoided there occur some telling observations such as "the administrative divisions of the Government of India which have been described above have done away with the old demarcations set up by the Hindu or Muslims". Similarly in the Appendix on *The Condition of India in 1906* (P. 517), the extinction of indigenous cotton and textile industry because of British trade intervention has been deplored. The current state of India in 1906 has been discussed under a wide variety of headings and statistics have been appended. A perusal of the list gives the idea of the comprehensive treatment which the authors sought to give to their subject. The list of the headings includes :

(1) Races and Languages
(2) Religions ;
(3) Education, Journalism, Literature and Arts ;
(4) Agriculture ;
(5) Forests ;
(6) Industry and Handicrafts ;

(7) Trade — Imports and Exports ;
(8) Railways ;
(9) Constitution of the Government of India — Central and Provincial Governments and Local Bodies.

The authors have taken great pains to arrive at a balanced view of all the historical personalities—Hindu, Muslim, Sikh and British. Slanders, controversies, undue praise, playing up of one historical personality against the other and partisan approach to events has been conscientiously avoided.

Aurangzeb, for instance, has been extolled for his simplicity and virtuous character. Due praise has been given to his courage and energy in war and his meticulous supervision of the administrative affairs of his Government. He has been compared with Akbar and declared equal with him in sagacity and industry. However, he has been slated for his narrow vision, mistreatment of Rajputs and Sikhs and his suspicious nature. The downfall of the Mughal dynasty has been ascribed to impersonal causes such as financial bankruptcy, weakening of administrative control and revolt of the Provincial Governors. Moral laxity and cultural decay have been cited as factors which contributed to the demise of Moghal rule.

It must be remembered that the idea of the rise and fall of nations and Governments on moral grounds was the pivot of Iqbal's historical outlook. Moral degeneration in his view meant "nafi-i-Khudi" which pushed an individual or a nation into the abyss of degradation. Moral decay saps the ability to create and as soon as a people lose their creative ability they fall on evil days.

Iqbal sincerely believed that the reason for the decline of the Muslim society lay in the human personality's loss of self-consciousness.

Iqbal's moralistic philosophy of history conforms to the Quran's interpretation of the Rise and Fall of Nations, Systems and Empires. The Holy Quran makes it clear that wrong doing of any kind is not conducive to the success or prosperity of any group of men "God is on the side of those who fear Him and do good".[1]

The Holy Quran further stresses that the historical process is selective :

"And when Abraham was tried with certain commands by his Lord, he fulfilled them. Wherefore, God said to him : I am about to make thee a leader of men. Abraham said : But what about my progeny ? God replied : My covenant does not include the wrong-doers."[2]

Iqbal had developed a dialectic conception of Good and Evil. According to his philosophy social progress depended upon the unity and struggle of these two opposite forces. But the creative activity of man brings about the triumph of the Good over Evil.

He saw a constant contrast in the world situation of the West and the East. The West's civilization was, in his opinion, on the road to ruin : and the East was awaiting its renovation and seeking its special path of historical progress. He believed in the inevitability of historical progress. Only Muslims in his words, see in history "the continuous, collective movement, a real, inevitable development in

1. xvi. 127. 2. ii. 124.

time."[3]

Having noted these broad principles let us turn now to specific instances in his poetry.

In his earlier poems he expressed intensely patriotic feelings. Patriotism he regarded as a "perfectly natural virtue which has a place in the moral life of man."[4]

An interesting idea in the early poems is that Nature stands majestic as the pageant of history moves on. For instance, "Himalaya stands young even though millenniums have passed by."[5]

He dwells on history in almost all of his patriotic poems. A representative poem is "Hindustani Bachon ka Qawmi Geet." In this poem the arrival of Greeks, Tartars, Arabs and Turks in India has been noted. Memory of Chishtie, the "Teacher of Truth", and Nanak, the "Singer of the Songs of Unity," has been evoked.

The entire structure of the well-known "Shikwa" and "Jawab-i-Shikwah" has been raised on the foundations of Muslim history. "Sar Guzasht-i-Adam" (The Story of Man, *Bang-i-Dara*, p. 80) reveals the universal history of man. The story of man, according to Iqbal, is characterised by two features : (*a*) perpetual change, (*b*) unending search for self-realisation. Man is prone to look at the surface only, yet if he would but turn his eye inward and search his heart he would find there residing the

3. *Reconstruction*, p. 14.

4. Iqbal, Presidential Address to the Annual Session of All-India Muslim Conference held in Lahore on 21, March 1930, in S. A. Vahid, Ed., *Thoughts and Reflections of Iqbal*, p. 197.

5. *Bang-i-Dara*, p. 3.

secret of existence.

Although I subjugated the Earth by my Reason,
Yet alas ! I could not discover the Secret of Existence,
At last when the eye, prone to see the surface only, opened,
I found it (the Secret of Existence) residing in the closet of my heart.[6]

Self-discovery (self-consciousness, *isbat-i-Khudi*) was the greatest moral duty of man. Iqbal praised Hindu Avatar Rama Chandra for his moral qualities, chivalry, purity and spirit of love.[7] For moral reasons again he condemned all forms of aggression and exploitation in ancient times or modern. In the fourth century B.C. Alexander of Macedon had waged imperialistic wars in Asia including the north-western provinces of the subcontinent. In contrast to the common trend of applauding Alexander's exploits and the tendency of text-book writers to dignify him with the title "Alexander the Great." Iqbal regarded the Greek King as no better than a blood-thirsty raider. In "Ayk Bahri Qazzaq Aur Sikandar" (Alexander and a Pirate), Alexander seizes the seafaring marauder and is weighing the nature of the punishment for his crimes. The pirate, however, objects that the Emperor with his judgment implicates himself and all his peers, and declares :

We shed blood alike, robbers are we—
You on land and I on sea.

A significant idea in Iqbal's philosophy of History is the impermanence of Brute Power and the continued existence of the masses. Several poems in *Darb-i-Kalim* depict the meteoric rise and fall of the empire-builder.

"Alexander stormed like lightning,

6. *Bang-i-Dara*, p. 81. 7. Ibid., p. 195.

> "And we all know that he suddenly died,"
>
> Or
>
> Nadir Shah robbed Delhi of its treasures and a single stroke of the sword put an end to his short history,"
>
> Or
>
> "There is no longer the Empire of Pervaiz in the world."[8]

Iqbal lamented the loss of Muslim power in India. The vision of Delhi, the seat of old Muslim culture, haunted his mind. In the poems "Mirza Ghalib" and "Dagh" in *Bang-i-Dara* he invariably turned to the memory of the old Muslim society in Delhi. The poem "Bilad-i-Islamiyah" in *Bang-i-Dara* reveals his commitment to Muslim History.

In "Shibli Awr Hali," Iqbal admired Hali for he was a man of action in the sense that he had probed the causes of the Muslims' downfall.

> Men of action probe the causes of events and find remedies for the misfortunes inflicted by fate.[9]

The House of Taimur fell from rule because it had lost "Hamiyyat" (self-respect, *Khudi*).

The poem "Ghulam Qadir Rohilla" tells a poignant story of the Mughal family's disgrace. The poet condemns the marauder Ghulam Qadir Rohilla as "cruel, vindictive fiend," but concludes that the terrible fate which overtook the royal family was a punishment for its moral incapacity.

> What was called "self-respect" has departed from the House of Taimur.[10]

In determining Iqbal's own place in the history of the subcontinent, one has first of all to consider his contribution to the historical evolution of the two-nation theory in India.

8. *Darb-i-Kalim*, pp. 157, 168.
9. *Bang-i-Dara*, p. 248.
10. Ibid., p. 245.

Islam entered India under Muhammad bin Qasim in 712 A.C. It must be borne in mind that Islam has a revolutionary impact on men and peoples. Those who accept Islam have their whole personality transformed, with a clear break with the past and a complete change of direction. Islam, with its distinct moral values and approach to the problems of life, binds its adherents into a compact ideological community.

Hinduism which has an assimilative character found Islam an invincible cultural force. A fundamental line of cleavage between Hindus and Muslims was almost immediately drawn. As early as A.D. 1001, the world-renowned savant al-Beruni, who had accompanied Sultan Mahmood Ghaznavi to India made the following observation regarding the Hindu attitude towards the Muslims in his book, *Kitab-ul-Hind.*

"All their fanaticism is directed against those who do not belong to them—against all foreigners. They call them *Malechha*, i.e. impure, and forbid having any connection with them, be it by inter-marriage or by any other kind of relationship or by sitting, eating or drinking with them, because thereby they would be polluted. They consider as impure anything which touches the fire and water of a foreigner, and no household can exist without these elements. They are not allowed to receive anybody who does not belong to them even if he wished it or is inclined to their religion. This renders connection between them quite impossible and constitutes the widest gulf between them and us."

Precisely the same relationship has existed between Hindus and Muslims during the last one thousand years. The two societies—Hindu and Muslim —like two streams, sometimes touched, but never merged, each following its separate course.

There were periods, however, when the consciousness of Muslims as a distinct nation was blurred. In comparatively more recent times we observe the phenomenon of proud Afghan chiefs fighting under the supreme command of a Hindu General Himu Baqqal against Akbar in the second battle of Panipat. Akbar himself unnerved by this experience and egged on by heretic advisers Mubarik, Faizi and Abul Fazl promulgated an eclectic religion, the "Din-i-Elahi", which immediately provoked storms and rebellions in all parts of India. The religion remained confined to a coterie of fawning nobles and neither Hindus nor Muslims saw any merit in it. Mujaddid-Alf-Thani and other Muslim savants had vigorously denounced the onslaught of heretical tendencies. The orthodox *ulama* made an effort to rehabilitate the prestige of Islam on the eve of Jehangir's succession to the throne, but the attitude of State towards Islam under Jehangir and his successor Shah Jahan remained by and large neutral.

The movement started by Akbar aimed at depoliticising Islam. Its adherents believed in a single nationhood for India. The onrush of this movement was effectively checked by Aurangzeb. He reaffirmed the distinct nationality of Musalmans in India.

In the clash of these two movements (which persisted right up to Partition in 1947), Iqbal was clearly on the side of Aurangzeb. Discussing in *Rumuz-i-Baikhudi* (The Mysteries of Selflessness) the personal fulfilment of the individual in society, Iqbal described

Aurangzeb as :

"He, the last arrow in our quiver left"
"In the affray of faith with unbelief"
and
"An Abraham in India's idol-house."

In his essay on "Muslim Community" Iqbal laid down the following principles of the dialectic movement in history :

"In primitive society where the struggle of existence is extremely keen and draws more upon man's physical rather than intellectual qualities, it is the valiant man who becomes an object of universal admiration and imitation ; when, however, the struggle relaxes and the peril is over, the valorous type is displaced, though not altogether, by what Giddings calls the convivial type, which takes a due share in all the pleasures of life and combines in itself the virtues of liberality, generosity and good fellowship. But these two types of character have a tendency to become reckless, and by way of reaction against them appears the third great type which holds up the ideal of self-control, and is dominated by a more serious view of life.

Analysing the course of modern Indian history in the light of this principle, Iqbal concluded that Alamgir's life and activity was the starting point in the growth of Muslim nationality in India.

"In so far as the evolution of the Muslim Society in India is concerned Taimur represented the first type, Babar combined the first and the second, Jehangir embodied pre-eminently the second ; while the third pre-shadowed in Alamgir, whose life and activity forms, in my opinion, the starting point in the growth of Muslim nationality in India. To me the ideal of character foreshadowed by Alamgir is essentially the Muslim type of character, and it must be the object of all our education to develop that type."[11]

11. *Census of India Report*, 1911, xiv, 162-164 ; also in Vahid, Ed., op. cit., pp. 379-80.

Aurangzeb died in 1707 and after a series of rapacious wars the British finally established their rule over the entire subcontinent in 1857. The Muslim community in India once again fell prey to an ideological dilemma. Recounting a childhood interview with M. A. Jinnah the Raja of Mehmoodabad writes:

> "I had just rerurned from school when my father took me to meet Mr. Jinnah and we sat talking on the terrace. He called me to his side and asked me about my studies. Then came the question : What are you, a Muslim first or an Indian first ?"[12]

This then was the dilemma. Sayyid Ahmad Khan tried to resolve the dilemma in the nineteenth century, but his main effort lay in the educational field. Since 1707 Iqbal was the first Muslim who reconstructed the ideology of Muslim nationhood. A Muslim was not Muslim because he belonged to a specific country, race or colour or spoke a particular tongue, but because he believed in the religious and social precepts of Islam. Only the religious idea of the unity of God, the Prophethood of Muhammad (peace and blessings of Allah be on him) and the social system of Islam constituted the basis of Muslim nationality. Islam abhorred territorial nationalism and believed in world unity on the basis of the Holy Qur'an. However, when Muslims were a minority in danger of being submerged, they were perfectly justified in demanding self-determination.[13]

He suggested in 1930 that "I would like to see the Panjab, North-West Frontier Province, Sindh

12. "Memories", Raja of Mehmoodabad in C. H. Philips, Ed., *Partition of India*, (London Allen and Unwin 1970), p. 385.

13. Letter to Jawaharlal Nehru in Vahid, op. cit., pp. 287-88 .

and Baluchistan amalgamated into a single State."[14]

Having defined the contours of a Muslim homeland in India, he actively engaged in the struggle for the achievement of this goal. His first concern was to forge unity among Muslim Leaders for an effective struggle against the Anglo-Hindu alliance in India.

In 1928, he had actively promoted the idea of holding an All-Parties Muslim Conference (later transformed into All-India Muslim Conference) at Delhi. The most important political organisation of the Muslims, the All-India Muslim League was in disarray during 1930-34. It was divided into factions, the principal ones being led by M. A. Jinnah and Mian Muhammad Shafi. During these years it was Iqbal who provided the ideological leadership to all India Muslims. He suggested the formation of a strong political organisation of the Muslims. It should be a truly mass party, having as its objective the political and cultural education of the masses.[15]

In the Punjab he clashed with the feudalists and succeeded in turning the Muslim League into a truly mass political party. In 1936, Iqbal invited Mr. M. A. Jinnah to inaugurate the League's Election Campaign and provided him with the first public stage in the Punjab.[16]

In his speeches and letters, Iqbal expressed full faith in the leadership of the Quaid-i-Azam. In 1930,

14. Presidential Address to All-India Muslim League. Allahabad, 1930.

15. Presidential Address, All-India Muslim Conference, Lahore, March 21. 1932.

16. Muslim League meeting outside Delhi Gate, Lahore, 11 Oct. 1936.

Iqbal had stated : "I lead no party, I follow no leader."[17]

In 1936 he was wholeheartedly willing to be led by Jinnah. In a joint statement with his friends Iqbal declared, "Our nation has full confidence in Jinnah's integrity and political judgment."[18]

In his Foreword to *Letters of Iqbal to Jinnah*, the Quaid-i-Azam gratefully acknowledged "the support that I obtained through the sincere and patriotic and selfless activities of many friends like Sir Mohammad Iqbal". Further on the Quaid-i-Azam wrote :

> "It was a great achievement for the Muslim League that its lead came to be acknowledged by both the majority and minority provinces. Sir Mohammad Iqbal played a very conspicuous part, though not revealed to the public, in bringing about this consummation."

Though Iqbal did not live to see the historic Muslim League Session at Lahore in 1940, it was he who had suggested the holding of the session in Lahore in a letter to M. A. Jinnah on 21 June 1937. At Lahore in 1940 M.A. Jinnah made a public reaffirmation of faith in ideas which Iqbal had expressed at Allahabad ten years earlier. Iqbal was the architect of Muslim nationalism in India and an active warrior in the struggle for the freedom of the people of India. He gave a message of love and faith to the Hindus and other non-Muslim communities. Iqbal sincerely believed that the speedy liberation of India from the yoke of British Imperialism depended on

17. Presidential Address All-India Muslim League, Allahabad, 1930.

18. *The Civil and Military Gazette*, 9, May 1936 ; also Batalvi *Iqbal Ke Akhri Do Saal*, pp. 312-13.

an amicable understanding between Hindus and Muslims Addressing the whole of India, he wrote: "People of India, if you do not learn, you'll be no more"[19]

He was at all times concerned with the economic sufferings of the Muslim as well as Hindu masses under British colonial rule. In analysing the problems of India, he invariably took an historical approach. In his speech in the Punjab Legislative Council on 5 March, 1927, Iqbal denounced the British theory of State-ownership of land on historical grounds. The British theory that all land belonged to the Crown, Iqbal said, "was a barbarous theory" and that "neither in ancient India nor even in the days of the Mughals had the sovereign ever claimed universal ownership. We are told that the Mughals claimed such rights but the people of the Punjab owned and possessed the land of this country long before the race of Babur entered into history, the unmistakable lesson of which is that Crowns come and go, the people alone are immortal." To clinch his argument Iqbal then quoted two of his Persian verses:

Alexander is dead and gone, and so are his sword and the Imperial flag.

Gone are also the cities and the mines which yielded him the tribute. Why don't you regard the nations as more lasting than the kings.

Can you not see, Iran lives, but her Emperors have gone.

Iqbal was a relentless foe of imperialism, capitalism, feudalism, Godless communism and fascism and in his understanding of the political and economic

19. *Bang-i-Dara*, pp. 32, 136.

realities of the world he was one of the most progressive men in India.

On a world-wide level he made some solid suggestions. He pointed out that the West had implanted the State of Israel in the heart of Islam to keep the Middle East in her constant grip. He advised a reunion of the Turks and Arabs and believed that Turks could still play a vigorous role in countering the imperialistic designs in the Middle East. He warned that Asia and more especially Asian Muslims should never put faith in the League of Nations. They would do well to form an Eastern League of Nations.

In his speeches and writings Iqbal felt concerned about almost all the national and international movements of his day.

Iqbal believed in the solidarity of the Muslim people all over the world and most important of all he had full faith in the ultimate destiny of Islam as expressed in the Holy Qar'an :

> "Allah has promised to those of you who believe and do good that He will surely make them rulers in the earth as He made those before them rulers and that He will establish for them their religion which He has chosen for them and that He will surely give them security in exchange after their fear."[20]

20 xxiv. 55

Bibliography

Abdul Hakim, Khalifa, Dr., *Islam and Communism* : Lahore, Institute of Islamic Culture, 1951.

Abdul Razzaq, *Kulliyat-i-Iqbal* : Hyderabad, 1923.

Agha Khan, *Memoirs* : London, 1953.

Ahmed, Sh. Mahmood, *The Pilgrimage of Eternity* : Lahore, Institute of Islamic Culture, 1961.

Arberry, A. J., *Complaint and Answer* : Lahore, Sh. Mohammad Ashraf, 1955.

———*The Mysteries of Selflessness* : London, John Murray, 1953.

———*The Tulip of Sinai* : London, The Royal India Society, 1947.

Batalvi, Ashiq Hussain, *Iqbal Kay Akhri Do Saal* : Karachi, 1961.

Chishti, Yusuf Salim, *Sharah Asrar-i-Khudi* : Lahore, 1954.

Coupland, R., *India, A Restatement* : London, Oxford, 1945.

Forester, E. M., *The Poetry of Iqbal* : "The Atheneum" 5—10 December, 1920.

Gibb, H. A. R., "Iqbal, Sir Muhammad" (1876—1938) in the *Dictionary of National Biography, 1931-1940* : London, Oxford, 1949.

Ikram, S. M., Dr., *Modern Muslim India and the Birth of Pakistan* : Lahore, Sh. Muhammad Ashraf, 1970.

Iqbal, Muhammad, Dr., *Asrar-i-Khudi* : Lahore, Sh. Ghulam Ali, 1959.

———*Bal-i-Jabril* : Lahore, Sh. Ghulam Ali, 1936.

———*Bang-i-Dara* : Lahore, Sh. Ghulam Ali, 1953.

———*Darb-i-Kalim* : Lahore, Sh. Ghulam Ali, 1959.

———*Ilm al-Iqtisad* : Karachi, Iqbal Academy, 1961.

———*Letters of Iqbal to Jinnah* : Lahore, Sh. Muhammad Ashraf, 1963.

———*Pas Cheh Bayad Kard Ay Aqwam-i-Sharq* : Lahore, Sh Ghulam Ali, 1958.

———*Payam-i-Mashriq* : Lahore, Sh. Ghulam Ali, 1958.

———*The Development of Metaphysics in Persia* : Lahore, Bazm-i-Iqbal, 1964.

———*The Reconstruction of Religious Thought in Islam* : Lahore, Sh. Muhammad Ashraf, 1958.

———& Lala Ram Prasad, *Tarikh-i-Hind* : Lahore, 1913.

Iqbal Singh, *The Ardent Pilgrim* : London, Longmans Green, 1951.

Jafri, Ali Sardar, *Taraqqi Pasand Adab* : Aligarh, 1951.

Javaid Iqbal, *Stray Reflections* : Lahore, Sh. Ghulam Ali, 1961.

Jawaharlal Nehru, *Discovery of India* : New York, 1946.

Khan Muhammad Ahmad, *Iqbal Ka Siyasi Karnamah* : Karachi, 1952.

Kiernan, V. G., *Poems from Iqbal* : London, John Murray, 1955.

Malcolm Darling, Sir, *The Punjab Peasant* : London, Oxford, 1947.

Mehr, Ghulam Rasul and Dilawari, *Sarud-i-Raftah* : Lahore, Sh. Ghulam Ali, 1959.

Moreland, W. H., *India at the Death of Akbar* : London, 1920.

Muhammad Ashraf, Malik, *The Devils' Conference* : Lahore, 1951.

Nicholson, R. A., *The Secrets of the Self* : Lahore, Sh. Muhammad Ashraf, 1961.

Percival Griffiths, *The British Impact on India* : London, Frank Cass, 1955.

Qureshi, Ishtiaq Hussain, *The Struggle for Pakistan* : Karachi, 1965.

Rajendra Prasad, *India Divided* : Bombay, 1947.

Richard Symonds, *The Making of Pakistan* : London, Faber & Faber, 1951.

Romila Thapar, *A History of India* : Baltimore, 1966.

Saiyid, M. H., *Muhammad Ali Jinnah : A Political Study* : Lahore, Sh. Muhammad Ashraf, 1953.

Salik, Abdul Majeed, *Dhikr-i-Iqbal* : Lahore, Bazm-i-Iqbal, 1955.

Shamloo, *Speeches and Statements of Iqbal* : Lahore, Al-Manar Academy, 1945.

Taj-ud-Din, Pir, *Iqbal's Political Career* : Lahore, Daily "The Pakistan Times", April 21, 1951.

Thomas Arnold, *The Faith of Islam* : London, 1928.

Vahid. S. A., *Iqbal—His Art and Thought* : London, 1959.

———*Thoughts & Reflections of Iqbal* : Lahore, Sh. Muhammad Ashraf, 1964.

Waheed-uz-Zaman, *Towards Pakistan* : Lahore, Publishers United Ltd., 1964.

Wahid-ud-Din, Syed Faqir, *Ruzgar-i-Faqir* : Karachi, 1966.

Index